John Medows Rodwell

The Prophecies of Isaiah

Translated from the Hebrew

John Medows Rodwell

The Prophecies of Isaiah
Translated from the Hebrew

ISBN/EAN: 9783337419431

Printed in Europe, USA, Canada, Australia, Japan

Cover: Foto ©Lupo / pixelio.de

More available books at **www.hansebooks.com**

THE PROPHECIES OF ISAIAH.

Translated from the Hebrew

BY

J. M. RODWELL, M.A.,

OF GONVILLE AND CAIUS COLLEGE, CAMBRIDGE; RECTOR OF ST.
ETHELBURGA, LONDON; TRANSLATOR OF THE KORAN
AND OF THE BOOK OF JOB; ETC., ETC.

SECOND EDITION.

LONDON:
FREDERIC NORGATE,
7, KING STREET, COVENT GARDEN;
WILLIAMS & NORGATE, 20, FREDERICK STREET, EDINBURGH.

1886.

TO

THE RIGHT HONOURABLE

WILLIAM EWART GLADSTONE,

Prime Minister of England,

THIS TRANSLATION

IS (BY HIS PERMISSION) DEDICATED

WITH SINCEREST RESPECT

BY

THE TRANSLATOR.

ERRATUM.

Page 96, line 13, punctuate and read—

'Protect this city.' (And Isaiah said: 'Let them
'bring a cake of figs, and let them bind to the boil,
'that he may live.' For Hezekiah said: 'What is
'the sign that I shall go up to the house of Yahveh?')
'And this the sign, &c.'

PREFACE.

THE object of the translator, in the following pages, is to present the utterances of the Prophet Isaiah in a form as nearly as possible identical with that in which they met the eye of those to whom they were originally addressed. He has therefore aimed on the one hand to be strictly literal and faithful to the Hebrew text, even at the cost of occasional roughness and baldness of expression, while, on the other, he has retained the parallelisms which are a distinguishing feature of all Hebrew poetry, and which, by the expansion of a primary idea into two or more varied forms, enable the writer not only to emphasize his statement, but to a great extent to become his own interpreter.

The translator has adhered throughout to the common Masoretic text with reference both to the order of the chapters and to its readings, with the exception of an occasional preference of the *Keri* to the *Chethib*, but without adopting in any case the conjectural emendations of modern scholars. It must, however, be admitted that the chapters admit of an arrangement more closely in harmony with the events which occurred during the reign of the various princes under whom Isaiah wrote, between the last year of Uzziah in B.C. 758, and the accession of Manasseh in B.C. 698. Judging from the analogy of other prophetic writings, it would seem as if the Book of Isaiah would more naturally commence with the introductory vision of chapter vi., while chapters xiii., xiv. 1—27, xix., xxi. 1—10, should follow, instead of preceding, chapters xxiv.—xxvii. At any rate, it is agreed by critics, both foreign and English, that the existing order of the prophecies is not strictly chronological, although the deviations from accuracy are not considerable. It will be sufficient in connection with this point to observe that some commentators, as Havernick, Gesenius, and Dr. Davidson, have proposed to divide the whole Book into four smaller portions, *viz.*, (1) chapters i—xiii : (2) chapters xiii—xxiii : (3) chapters xxiv—xxxv, treating the historical and prose chapters, xxxvi—xxxix as a kind of of appendix, adopted and incorporated with certain modifications from the national chronicles : and (4) chapters xl—lxvi : while other critics, as Ewald and Delitzsch, subdivide the Book to a still greater extent, and suppose the existence of several authors and editors, at different periods. To prosecute, however, this difficult and thorny subject, would be wholly inconsistent with the necessary limits of a preface, as well as with the translator's main object as above stated. It will be sufficient here to remark that chapters xl—lxvi have been assigned to another writer than the Isaiah of the previous prophecies, principally on the ground of difference of style and expression as well as of subject matter.

A translation will naturally take much of its tone and colour from the views which the translator himself may happen to entertain of prophecy in general, and of the extent to which he regards the writings of any particular prophet as penetrated by the Messianic idea. He might thus be able to translate according to some preconceived theory or bias, and often to stamp his own theological views on the very front of his version. If, for instance, he should be persuaded that the Prophecies of Isaiah, down to the minutest particulars, have immediate and primary reference to *passing* events, and at the same time contain implied references to *coming* events in the history of the Jewish people and of humanity at large—that whatever was spoken by Isaiah of Jerusalem—of the Righteousness, or righteous and faithful dealings of God with Israel, resulting in national *Prosperity*, as in ch. lxii. 12—of their *Salvation*, or deliverance from Babylon—of *Cyrus* as its instrument—of the *Goel* i.e., Vindicator, Liberator or Redeemer, as one who ransoms, brings back into freedom, and so restores, a lost inheritance—of *the Servant* or *servants* of God as prophetic announcers of deliverance—not only admits of application to the Christian dispensation at large, but was so intended—he would naturally translate in accordance with his prepossessions, believing that words which to Isaiah himself must have been little more than a dim intuition, assume the proportion of divine enlightenment when taken in connection with the Evangelic History. At the same time he would find himself burdened with the difficulty of doing justice to this twofold aspect of his author, and in danger of bringing either the Present or the Future into undue prominence by his choice of words and renderings.

A translator, moreover, may see in the Prophecies of Isaiah nothing more than the utterances of a pure patriotism, vague but lofty hopes of a brighter future, interspersed with dark pictures of the sufferings to which the faithful servants of God, whether as individuals, or as a prophetic order, or as a faithful remnant among the people, would be subjected. He might see in them merely a reflection of the stormy times which ushered in and caused the decadence of the Jewish nation, and the rejection of an unwelcome message, which would draw down upon the prophet bitter persecution. To such a translator Isaiah would be little more than the patriot statesman, or the stern moralist filled with a boldness which enabled him to rebuke the sinful, whether princes or people, to strengthen the vacillating and encourage the faint-hearted. He would see in him one of those who stood against their age and the spirit of the world—never despairing of better times— a devout adorer of the God of his Fathers,—full of Faith in a Divine superintendence, and thus enabled to look through all the clouds that obscured the present, to a bright but unknown future. Such a translator would of course translate in accordance with his literalistic views.

But whatever opinions the translator of Isaiah may hold, he ought to be especially on his guard against the loose, ornate, and paraphrastic style which has so greatly disfigured the earlier, as well as against that tendency to a mystic pietism, which finds the ideal, spiritual and supersensible, where nothing but passing events and matters of fact were intended by the author, so characteristic of some recent translations.

The translations of Gesenius and of Ewald with their accompanying commentaries, especially that of Gesenius, may be studied with the greatest advantage. A considerable amount of learning may be found in the notes appended to the version of the late Dr. Henderson, but the version itself is very faulty. He leans far too strongly to the Messianic interpretation.

The accuracy and trustworthiness of the historical portions of the Prophet Isaiah may be illustrated by an extract from my translation of the Cuneiform text of a slab belonging to the Koyunjik Bulls in the British Museum, published in the *Records of the Past*, vol. vii., and and commonly known as the Sennacherib Inscription. It says (v.22), "The Governors and the population of the city Ekron, who Padi their king (23) an ally of Assyria with a chain of iron had bound, and to Hezekiah king of Judah had delivered him—them the shadows of death overwhelmed. . . . Hezekiah king of Judah did not submit to my yoke ; (28) Forty-six of his cities . . . I plundered. Himself I made like a caged bird in the midst of Jerusalem—the city of his royalty (29). Garrison towers against him I raised. . . . (30). Hezekiah himself, the fear of the approach of my majesty (31) overwhelmed, and the soldiers whom he had caused to enter Jerusalem his royal city. He consented to the payment of tribute, 30 talents of gold, 800 talents of silver."

The Bel and Nebo of Isasah xlvi. 1, are mentioned together as thus addressed by Cyrus, on the Babylonian Cylinder described in the *Trans. Soc. Bibl. Archæol.*, vol. vii, p. 139 sqq., "That the length of my days they should fulfil, and that they should bless the law of my destiny, I addressed Bel and Nebo every day."

NOTE.

N.B.—The asterisk (*) occasionally found in the following pages, indicates the use, in the Hebrew, of a paronomasia,—*assonance*, or play upon words of similar sound but different meaning, which could not be reproduced in translation.

The reader of Isaiah should be apprized that the *time*, past, present, or future, implied in Hebrew verbs, is often to be gathered from the context, and that in some cases each of the tenses is employed with equal propriety. *Vide* GESENIUS, *Grammar*, ch. iii., on the *Syntax of the Hebrew Verb*.

THE PROPHECIES OF ISAIAH.

CHAPTER I. 1—4.

The great arraignment. (Ewald). Complaints of the universal corruption and degeneracy of the people: with intimations of impending judgments, and the promise of a reformation and return to primitive purity and prosperity.

Vision of Isaiah, son of Amos, which he saw concerning Judah and Jerusalem, in the days of Uzziah, Jotham, Ahaz, Hezekiah, Kings of Judah.

    Hearken, O heavens, and give ear, O earth,
    For Yahveh speaks!
    " I have reared and brought up sons,
    " And they have broken away from me!
    " An ox knows his owner,
    " And an ass his master's crib :—
    " Israel knows not,
    " My people doth not consider! "

Ah sinful nation!* guilt-laden people!
Seed of transgressors! sons that act corruptly!
They have forsaken Yahveh,
Have disdained Israel's Holy One,
Are gone away backward!

CHAPTER I. 5—12.

Why, increasing revolt, will ye still be smitten?
Every head sickens and every heart is faint;
From sole of foot even to head—no soundness in it—
But wound and weal and festering sore:
They have not been pressed out, nor bound up,
Nor softened with oil.
Your land— a desolation!
Your cities burned with fire!
Your soil aliens devour it in your presence—
Even a desolation, like an overthrow by aliens!
And Zion's daughter is left
Like a hut in a vineyard,
Like a lodge in a cucumber field,
Like a besieged city!
Had not Yahveh of Hosts left us a remnant,
We had within a little been as Sodom,
We had been like to Gomorrah!

Judges of Sodom, hear the word of Yahveh!
People of Gomorrah, give ear to *the* teaching [Torah]
  of our Elohim.

Wherefore a multitude of your sacrifices to me? saith
  Yahveh:
I am sated with burnt offerings of rams and fat of
  fatlings,
And *in* blood of bullocks and lambs and he goats I
  delight not.
When ye come to behold my face,
Who hath required this at your hands—to tread my
  courts!

Chapter I. 13—21.

Bring no more an oblation of vanity,
Incense that is an abomination to me—
New moon and Sabbath and calling of assembly—
I cannot endure wickedness and festival:
Your new moons and your set days my soul hates,
They have become a weight upon me,
I am weary of bearing *it*.
And when ye spread forth your palms,
I will hide mine eyes from you:
Even if ye make many prayers I listen not—
Your hands are full of blood.
Wash ye, purify yourselves,
Put away *the* evil of your doings from before mine eyes,
Cease to do wrong, learn to do good:
Seek judgment, set right *the* oppressor,
To orphan do justice, for widow plead.

Come now, let us close our dispute, saith Yahveh;
"Though your sins be like scarlet, they shall be white like snow;
"Though they be red like crimson, they shall be like wool.
"If ye be willing and hearken, ye shall eat *the* good of the land,
"But if ye refuse and rebel, by *the* sword shall ye be eaten.
"For Yahveh's mouth has said *it*."

How is a faithful city become an harlot,
She that was full of justice!

Chapter I. 21—31.

Righteousness did abide in her—but now, murderers !
Thy silver is become dross,
Thy wine weakened with water ;
Thy rulers are unruly,* and comrades of robbers,
Every one loves a bribe, and hurries after rewards,—
To orphan they do no justice,
Nor comes *the* cause of widow to them.

Therefore—a voice from Yahveh of Hosts, Israel's
  mighty one :—
Ha ! I will get me ease through mine adversaries,
And I will be avenged* on my foes ;
And I will bring back my hand upon thee,
And smelt out thy dross as *with* lye,
And take away all thy alloy,
And bring back thy judges as at first,
And thy counsellors as at *the* beginning.
After this thou shalt be called,
Watchtower of righteousness, Faithful city ;
Through justice shall Zion be preserved,
And they that turn in her, through righteous dealing,
But a destruction of renegades and sinners together !
And they who forsake Yahveh shall be consumed.
For they shall be ashamed of the terebinths in which
  ye found pleasure,
And ye shall blush for the gardens which ye chose ;
Yea, ye shall be like a terebinth whose leaf withers,
And like a garden which has no water ;
And the strong one becomes tow,
And his work a spark,

CHAPTER I. 5—12.

And they both burn together,
And no one quenches.

CHAPTERS II. III. IV.

CHAPTER II. 1—4.

Mount Zion is to be a centre of religious unity. Present confidence in sorcery and idols. The pride and extravagance of women. Future restoration, fertility and security.

The word which Isaiah, son of Amoz, saw concerning Judah and Jerusalem :
" And it comes to pass in the after-days
" That *the* mountain of Yahveh's house
" Shall be fixed on *the* top of the mountains,
" And exalted above *the* hills :
" And all the nations flow unto it,
" And many peoples set forth and say,
" Come, let us go up to Yahveh's mount,
" To *the* house of Jacob's God,
" And let Him teach us of His ways,
" And we will walk in His paths :
" For out of Zion shall a teaching [Torah] go forth,
" And from Jerusalem *the* word of Yahveh.
" Then He judges among the nations,
" And decides for many peoples ;
" And they beat their swords into ploughshares,
" And their spears into pruning hooks :

Chapter II. 4—12

"Nation lifts not up sword against nation,
" And they learn war no more. "
Come, house of Jacob,
And let us walk in *the* light of Yahveh.
For Thou hast abandoned thy people. *the* house of Jacob,
Because they are filled from the East,
And are cloud-observers like *the* Philistines,
And strike bargains with sons of aliens :
And his land is filled with silver and gold,
And to his treasures there is no end ;
And his land is filled with horses,
And to his chariots there is no end ;
And his land is full of vain-gods,
To *the* work of their hands they do reverence,
To that which their fingers have wrought ;
And *the* mean man bows down,
And *the* great man abases himself,
And thou forgivest them not.
Enter into *the* rock and hide thee in *the* dust
From before *the* terror of Yahveh and from *the* splendour of his majesty :—
Man's haughty eyes are humbled
And *the* loftiness of men is bowed down,
And Yahveh alone is exalted in that day.

For Yahveh of Sabaoth hath a day
Against all that is proud and lofty,
And against all that is uplifted, that it be brought low ;
And against all cedars of the Lebanon, the lofty and the uplifted,

Chapter II. 13—22.

And against all oaks of the Bashan ;
And against all the lofty mountains,
And against all the uplifted hills,
And against every high tower,
And against every fenced wall,
And against all ships of Tarshish,
And against all delightful sights,
And man's highness is bowed down,
And *the* loftiness of mortals is brought low,
And Yahveh alone is exalted in that day.

And the vain-gods—*the* whole shall pass away ;
And they go into caverns of rocks and into holes of *the* ground
From before the terror of Yahveh,
And from *the* splendour of His majesty,
When He uprises to affright the earth.*
In that day shall the man cast away
His vain-gods of silver and his vain-gods of gold,
Which they had made for him to worship,
To moles and to bats :
To go into clefts of the rocks
And into rents of the crags,
From before *the* terror of Yahveh
And from *the* splendour of His majesty
When He upriseth to affright the earth.

Cease ye from the earth-born,
In whose nostrils is *but* a breath,
For in what is he to be accounted of ?

Chapter III. 1—9.

For behold, the Lord Yahveh of Sabaoth
Withdraws from Jerusalem and Judah,
Stay and staff,
All stay of bread, and all stay of water,
Champion and man of war,
Judge and prophet, and diviner and elder,
Captain of fifty and man of lofty bearing,
And counsellor and skilled labourer and adept
    in charms.
And I will make youths their princes,
And *with* caprice will they rule over them ;
And the people shall be oppressed,
Man by man, and each by his neighbour.
They will outrage—the youth, *the* aged,
And the mean man, him who is to be honoured;
For a man will lay hold on his brother *in* his father's
    house—
—" Thou hast raiment,
" Thou shalt be our ruler,
And let this ruin be under thy hand. "
On that day shall he lift up *his voice*,
" I will not be a healer,
" And in my house *is* neither bread nor raiment ;
" Ye shall not make me a ruler of *the* people. "
For Jerusalem totters and Judah falls,
Because their tongue and their doings are against
    Yahveh,
To provoke *the* eyes of His glory.
The shew of their countenance witnesses against them ;
And they proclaim their sin like Sodom ; they hide *it* not,

THE PROPHECIES OF ISAIAH.

CHAPTER III. 9—18.

Alas, for them ! for to themselves they have requited evil.
Say ye *of* the righteous, "*it is* well,"
For *the* fruit of their deeds shall they eat :
Alas for *the* wicked ! " ill ! "
For unto him *the* desert of his hands shall be rendered.
My people ! a child is his oppressor,
And women lord it over him :
My people ! thy guides are causing to err,
And they swallow up thy pathways.

Yahveh is stationed to plead,
And stands to judge peoples ;
Yahveh will enter into judgment
With *the* elders of his people and its princes :
" For ye have eaten up the vineyard,
Plunder of the poor is in your houses.
What mean ye that ye crush my people,
And grind *the* face of *the* poor ? "
An oracle of *the* Lord Yahveh Sabaoth.

And Yahveh saith,
Because Zion's daughters are haughty,
And walk with outstretched neck and leering eyes,
Walking and mincing as they walk,
And tinkling with their feet ;
Therefore will Adonai make bald *the* crown of Zion's daughters,
And Yahveh will lay bare their shame.
In that day Adonai will strip away,

Chapter III. 18—IV. 1.

The ornaments of the anklets and the network and the crescents,
The ear-drops and the bracelets and the veils,
The tires and the stepchains and the girdles,
And the perfume boxes and the amulets,
The signet-rings and the nose-rings,
The rich dresses and the mantles,
And the cloaks and the purses,
The mirrors and the linen vests,
And the turbans and the shawls.
And it comes to pass *that* instead of fragrance there shall be rottenness,
And instead of a cincture a rope;
And instead of a work of curls, baldness;
And instead of a wide mantle, a girding with sackcloth;
A brand instead of beauty.
Thy men fall by *the* sword,
And thy mighty men in war;
And her gates lament and wail,
And she sits, emptied, upon *the* ground.
And seven women lay hold on one man in that day, saying,
"Our own bread will we eat,
And with our own garments will we be clad;
Only let us be called by thy name;
Take away our reproach."
In that day shall *the* upgrowth of Yahveh be for splendour and for glory,
And *the* fruit of the land, for excellency and for beauty,

CHAPTER IV. 2—6.

To *the* escaped of Israel.
And it comes to pass that whosoever is left in Zion
And remains in Jerusalem,
Shall be called holy,
Every one written down for life in Jerusalem,
When Adonai hath washed away the filth of Zion's daughters,
And from her midst has purged the blood of Jerusalem,
With blast of judgment and with blast of burning.
And, upon *the* whole station of Mount Zion
And upon her places of assembly,
Yahveh will create a cloud by day and smoke,
And a brightness of flaming fire by night;
Yea, over all *the* glory *shall be* a covering,
And it shall be a pavilion for shade from heat by day,
And for a covert and for a refuge from storm and from rain.

CHAPTER V. 1—2.

The ungrateful and disappointing vineyard. The Assyrian invasion.

Let me now sing concerning my beloved,
A song of my Love about his vineyard.
My beloved had a vineyard
Upon a hill-top, son of fatness :
And he digged it and cleared it of stones,
And planted it with *the* Sorek-*vine*,
And in the midst of it he built a tower,

Chapter V. 2—9.

And also hollowed out a wine-vat in it;
And he hoped that it would bear grapes,
But it bore wild-grapes!
And now, Inhabitants of Jerusalem and men of Judah,
Judge, I pray, between me and my vineyard.
What *was there* yet to do for my vineyard that I have not done in it?
Why, when I hoped that *it* should bring forth grapes,
Brought *it* forth wild-grapes?
And now, I pray, let me acquaint you,
What I will do to my vineyard—
Taking away its fence that it become a pasture,
Demolishing its wall that it become downtrodden:
And I will make it a waste;
It shall not be pruned and it shall not be weeded,
And thorn and thistle springs up;
And on the clouds will I lay a charge
To rain no rain upon it.
For *the* vineyard of Yahveh Sabaoth is *the* house of Israel,
And *the* men of Judah His delightsome plant;
And He hoped for justice, but lo! bloodshed,*
For equity, but lo! an outcry.*

Woe to those who join house to house,
Who lay field to field till room fails,
And ye have to dwell alone in *the* midst of the land!
In Mine ears *saith* Yahveh Sabaoth,
Surely many houses shall become a desolation,
Great and fair ones without inhabitant;

Chapter V. 10—19.

For ten acres of vineyard shall yield *but* a single bath,
And seed of an homer shall yield an ephah.
Woe to those who rise at dawn to follow after strong drink,
Who are late at even *till* wine inflame them:
And lyre and cymbal, timbrel and pipe and wine *are in* their revel,
But the work of Yahveh they regard not,
And *the* operation of His hands they do not behold.
Therefore is My people led unawares into exile,
And his nobles *become* men of famine,
And his riotous throng, parched with thirst.
Therefore Sheol enlarges her appetite,
And opens her mouth without limit,
And down go her glory and her riotous throng,
And her uproar and he that was joyous within her;
And *the* mean man is bowed down, and the *great* man is brought low,
And *the* eyes of *the* haughty are brought low,
But Yahveh Sabaoth is exalted through justice,
And the holy God is hallowed through His righteous dealing.
Then feed *the* lambs as on their own pasture,
And aliens eat *the* wastes of *the* rich.

Woe to those who draw on the punishment *of guilt* with cords of ungodliness,
And sin as with traces of a wain;
Who say let Him speed, let Him hasten on His work,
To the intent that we may see it;

CHAPTER V. 19—26.

And let *the* purpose of Israel's Holy one draw nigh
and come that we may know it!

Woe to those *who* call evil good and good evil,
Who put darkness for light and light for darkness;
Who put bitter for sweet and sweet for bitter!

Woe to *the* wise in their own eyes
And prudent in their own esteem!

Woe to the heroes in drinking wine,
Who declare *the* wicked righteous for a bribe;
And men of prowess in mingling strong drink;
And take away *the* righteousness of *the* righteous
from him.

Therefore as tongue of fire devours stubble,
And burning grass sinks down *in the flame,*
So their root shall be as rottenness,
And their blossom shall go up as dust;
For they have despised the instruction of Yahveh
Sabaoth,
And the utterance of Israel's Holy One have they
scorned.

Wherefore *the* anger of Yahveh is kindled against His
people,
And He stretches out His hand against him,
And He smites him, and the mountains quake,
And their carcases are like sweepings in mid-streets.
For all this His anger turns not back,
But His hand is stretched out still.

And He raises a standard to far off nations,

CHAPTER V. 26—30.

And from *the* ends of the earth He hisses to him,
And lo! with speed He lightly comes;
None is weary, and none stumbles therein,
He slumbers not and sleeps not,
The girdle of His loins is not loosed,
And *the* thong of His sandals is not broken:—
Whose arrows are sharpened,
And all His bows bent;
His horses' hoofs are counted like stone,
And His wheels like a whirlwind.
He has a roar like a lioness,
And like young lions He roars,
And growls and seizes on prey,
And bears it off, and there is none to rescue!
And in that day, one roars against Him as *the* roaring of a sea;
And if one look to *the* land,
Behold darkness, *and* distress,
And light is dark through its clouds.

CHAPTER VI. 1—3.

Call of Isaiah to the Prophetic office. His message to the Jewish nation.

In the year that King Uzziah died, I saw the Lord sitting on a high and uplifted throne, and His train filling the temple—Seraphim standing above Him, each with six wings; with two he covered his face, and with two he covered his feet and with two he flew. And one

Chapter VI. 3—11.

called to the other and said,

    Holy, Holy, Holy, is Yahveh Sabaoth,
    | *The* fulness of the whole earth is, His glory.

And *the* foundations of the thresholds quaked at the voice of him that cried, and the house was filled with smoke. Then said I, woe is me! surely I perish : for I am a man of unclean lips, and I dwell amid a people of unclean lips ; for mine eyes have seen the King, Yahveh Sabaoth ! Then one of the Seraphim flew to me, and in his hand a hot stone which he had taken with tongs from off the altar : and he touched my mouth and said : " Lo, this hath touched thy lips and thine iniquity is taken away, and thy sin is forgiven. " Also, I heard the voice of the Lord saying,

    Whom shall I send
    And who will go for us ?

Then said I, " Behold *here am* I, send me. " And He said,

  Go, and say to this people,
  " Hear on, but understand not,
  And see on, but perceive not ;
  Make fat this people's heart,
  And its ears make heavy and its eyes besmear,
  Lest it see with its eyes and hear with its ears,
  And lest its heart understand, and it turn, and be healed. "

Then said I, O Lord, how long?
And He said, Until cities be waste without inhabitant,
  And houses without men,

Chapter VI. 11—13.

And the ground be waste, desolate,
And Yahveh have removed men afar,
And large the deserted places in *the* midst of the land.
And should there still be a tenth therein,
It likewise would be burned :
Like a terebinth and like an oak,
At whose felling remains a stem ;
So their stem *shall be* a holy seed.

CHAPTERS VII. 1—IX. 7.

Chapter VII. 1—4.

Consternation of Ahaz in prospect of the siege of Jerusalem by the forces of Syria and Israel. Allegorical or typical signs assuring him of deliverance. The Assyrian invasion.

And it came to pass in *the* days of Ahaz son of Jotham, son of Uzziah king of Judah, that Rezin king of Aram, with Pekah son of Remaliah, king of Judah, came up to Jerusalem for war against it, but was not able to wage the war against it. And it was announced to the house of David saying, " Aram is resting *in alliance* on Ephraim ;" and his heart shook, and *the* heart of his people, as trees of a forest shake before *the* wind. Then said Yahveh to Isaiah, " Go forth now to meet Ahaz, thou and REMNANT-SHALL-RETURN thy son, at *the* end of *the* conduit of the upper pool, at *the* causeway of the fuller's field, and thou shalt say to him :

Chapter VII. 4—14.

Be wary and be still:
Fear not neither let thy heart be faint,
Because of these two stumps of the smoking brands,
At *the* hot wrath of Rezin and Aram, and Remaliah's son:
Because Aram has plotted mischief against thee,
With Ephraim and *the* son of Remaliah, saying,
"Let us go up against Judah and alarm it,
And let us break it open for ourselves,
And let us make king in the midst of it the son of Tabel:"
Thus saith *the* Lord Yahveh,
It shall not stand and it shall not be:
For the head of Aram is Damascus
And *the* head of Damascus, Rezin;
Yet within sixty-five years shall Rezin be broken,
That it be not a people:
And *the* head of Ephraim is Samaria,
And *the* head of Samaria *the* son of Remaliah;
If ye do not hold-fast, verily ye shall not stand-fast.*

And Yahveh spoke again to Ahaz, saying,
"Ask for thyself a sign from Yahveh thine Elohim,
Ask it in the depth, or in the height above."
But Ahaz said, "I will not ask, neither will I make trial of Yahveh."
Then said he, "Hear ye now, house of David:
Is it too little for you to weary out men,
That ye weary out my Elohim also?
Therefore the Lord Himself will give you a sign:

Chapter VII. 14—22.

Behold the maiden conceives and bears a son,
And calls His name GOD-WITH-US.
Curdled-milk and honey shall He eat,
When He knows how to refuse *the* bad and to choose *the* good;
For ere yet the boy shall know,
How to refuse *the* bad and to choose *the* good,
The land, at whose two kings thou art disquieted, shall be deserted.
Yahveh will bring upon thee,
Days such as have not come,
Since *the* day that Ephraim revolted from Judah,
—The King of Assyria.

And in that day it comes to pass,
That Yahveh shall hiss for *the* flies which *are* at *the* end of Egypt's rivers,
And for *the* bees in *the* land of Assyria;
And they come and light, all of them,
On *the* desolate valleys and on *the* clefts of the rocks,
And on all *the* thickets and on all *the* pastures.
In that day *the* Lord will shave
With razor hired beyond *the* River,
By the King of Assyria,
The head and hair of the feet,
And the beard too shall it take away.
And it comes to pass in that day,
That a heifer *and* two sheep *only* can a man maintain;
Yet it comes to pass that from *the* full supply of milk
He shall eat curdled milk.

Chapter VII. 22—25.

For every one shall eat only curdled milk and honey,
Who is left within the land.
And so it is in that day, that there shall be in every place,
Wherein were a thousand vines
At a thousand *pieces* of silver,
—for thorns and for briars shall it be :
With arrows and with bow shall *a man* go thither,
For all the land shall be briars and thorns,
And *as for* all the hills which were cleared with hoe,
Thither comes not *the* fear of thorns and briars,
But it becomes *a place* for sending forth of oxen,
And for sheep to tread.

Chapter VIII. 1—6.

And Yahveh said to me : Take thee a large tablet and inscribe on it with *the* stylus of *the* common people, concerning "PLUNDER-QUICKLY-PREY-SWIFTLY," and that I should take to me trustworthy witnesses Uriah the Priest, and Zechariah *the* son of Jeberechiah. Then I had connexion with the Priestess, and she conceived and bare a son ; and Yahveh said to me, Call his name PLUNDER-QUICKLY-PREY-SWIFTLY : for ere the boy know *how* to cry 'my father' and 'my mother' *Men* will bear away the riches of Damascus and the prey of Samaria before *the* king of Assyria. And Yahveh spoke to me again saying :

Because this people scorns

Chapter VIII. 6—14.

The softly flowing waters of the Shiloah
And rejoices in Rezin and *the* son of Remaliah,
Therefore behold, Adonai brings up upon them,
The waters of the river, the strong and the great,
—The king of Assyria and all his glory—
And it rises up above all its channels
And passes over all its banks,
And it sweeps into Judah and overflows the floods—
To *the* neck it reaches ;
And *the* spreading of it wings cover
The full-breadth of Thy land o GOD-WITH-US.
Be enraged ye peoples—yet ye break down—
And give ear all ye far off lands :
Gird yourselves, yet ye break down,
Gird yourselves, yet ye break down :—
Purpose a purpose, yet it shall be frustrated—
Decree a decree, yet it shall not stand,
For GOD-IS-WITH-US.
For thus spake Yahveh to me, *and* strong was His hand *upon me,*
And warned me not to walk in the way of this people,
Saying : Say ye not that all is conspiracy,
Which this people declares to be a conspiracy,
Neither fear what they fear nor be dismayed.
Yahveh Sabaoth —Him reverence,
And let Him be your fear, and Him your dread :
And He will be to you for a sanctuary,
And *yet* a tripping-stone and for a rock of stumbling
To both houses of Israel,
For a snare and for a trap to *the* dwellers in Jerusalem,

Chapter VIII. 15—23.

And many among them stumble and fall,
And are broken and snared and caught.

Bind up a testimony,
Seal a precept [Torah], among my taught ones,
—And I will wait for Yahveh
Who hides His face from *the* house of Jacob,
And in Him I hope—
BEHOLD, I AND THE CHILDREN WHOM YAHVEH HAS
 GIVEN ME,
ARE FOR SIGNS AND FOR PORTENTS IN ISRAEL
FROM YAHVEH SABAOTH WHO DWELLS ON MOUNT ZION.
And when they shall say to you,
" Enquire of the necromancers and the wizards
Who gibber and who moan ;
Should not a people consult their Elohim ?
The dead concerning the living ?
Then, to *the* precept and to *the* testimony :
If they shall not speak according to this word,
It is because no dawn is on them ;
And *each* passes through *the land*
Hard pressed and famished ;
And it comes to pass that, when he shall be famished
 that he is also fretted,
And curses his king and his Elohim and looks up !
And if one look to *the* earth
Then lo ! anguish of darkness, dimness of trouble ;
And into gloom he is driven.
Yet there is not *ever* gloom where is *now* distress ;
As the former time brought into contempt

THE PROPHECIES OF ISAIAH.

CHAPTER IX. 1—7.

The land of Zebulun and *the* land of Naphtali,
So the latter has honoured
The way by the sea, beyond the Jordan, *the* district
   of the nations.
The people that walked in darkness,
Behold a great light ;
Dwellers in a land of death-shade,—
On them a light shines brightly.
Thou hast multiplied the nation,
Thou hast increased its joy !
They joy before thee like *the* joy in harvest,
And as men exult when they divide spoil !
For, the yoke of his burden, and the staff *which
   smote* his shoulder,
The rod of his task-master,
Hast Thou broken as *in the* day of Midian.
For every sandal of the sandalled in conflict
And garment rolled in blood,
Is for burning, food for fire.
For to us a Child is born,
To us a Son is given,
And on His shoulder is laid the rule
And *men* call His name
Wonderful-counsellor, Mighty-deity
Evermore-a-father, Prince-of-peace :
For enlargement of empire and for endless
   peace,
Upon David's throne and over his kingdom,
To stablish and to support it,
Through justice and through faithful dealing,

Chapter IX. 7.

Henceforth and for ever!
The zeal of Yahveh Sabaoth will perform this.

CHAPTERS IX. 8—X. 4.

Chapter IX. 8—14.

The fate of the Northern Kingdom.

Into Jacob has Adonai sent a message,
And into Israel has it lighted down;
And all *His* people know *it*,
Ephraim and dwellers in Samaria,
In pride and fullness of heart, declaring,
" Bricks are fallen, but with hewn stones we will build up;
Sycamores have been cut down, but with cedars will we replace them. "
Therefore will Yahveh strengthen the princes of Rezin against him,
And arm his foes;
Syria in front, and Philistines in rear,
And they will devour Israel with open mouth.

    For all this His anger is not turned away,
    And His hand is stretched out still.

But the people turn not to Him that smote them,
And Yahveh Sabaoth they seek not:
Therefore Yahveh will cut off from Israel head and tail,

Chapter IX. 14—X. 1.

Palm-branch and bulrush *in* a single day;
The ancient and the man of lofty bearing, he is the head,
And *the* false-teaching prophet, he is the tail;
And *the* leaders of this people seduce them,
And those who are led *by them* are swallowed up.
Therefore Adonai will not rejoice in their youth,
And their orphans and their widows he will not pity,
For every one is profane and an evil-doer,
And every mouth speaks folly.

   For all this his anger is not turned away,
   And his hand is stretched out still.

For wickedness burns like fire, .
Thorn and thistle it devours;
And in thickets of the forest it kindles,
And they roll up *in* a column of smoke.
Through *the* wrath of Yahveh Sabaoth is *the* land
    burnt up,
And the people are as fuel of fire:
No one will pity his brother.
For *a man* will snatch on *the* right hand and *yet* is
    hungry;
And devour on *the* left hand, yet is not satisfied;
They devour, each *the* flesh of his own arm :
—Manasseh Ephraim, and Ephraim Manasseh,
Both together against Judah.

   For all this his anger is not turned away,
   And his hand is stretched out still.

Woe to those who decree unrighteous decrees,
To scribes who put oppression on record,

Chapter X. 2—4.

To turn aside *the* feeble from judgment,
And to strip *their* right *from the* afflicted of My people,
That widows may be their prey,
And *that* they may plunder *the* orphans.
What then will ye do in *the* day of visitation,
And in a desolation that cometh from afar?
To whom will ye flee for succour?
And where will ye leave your glory?
Forsaken by Me they crouch among *the* captives,
And they shall fall among *the* slain.

> For all this his anger is not turned away,
> And his hand is stretched out still.

CHAPTERS X. 5—12.—XII. 6.

Chapter X. 5—7.

Woes against Asshur (Assyria), and Deliverance for the remnant of Jacob. Promises of National prosperity. Hymns of Thanksgiving.

Woe to Asshur, rod of my anger,
And a staff in whose hand is my indignation!
Against a wicked nation I send him,
And against people of my wrath I give him charge,
To take spoil and seize on prey,
And to make it a trampling like mire in the streets.
But he—he means not thus,
And his heart—not thus does it purpose,

THE PROPHECIES OF ISAIAH.

Chapter X. 7—14.

For to destroy is in his heart,
And to cut off nations not a few.
"For," saith he, "are not my princes wholly kings?
Is not Calno as Carchemish?
Is not Hamath as Arpad?
Is not Samaria as Damascus?
As my hand has reached the kingdoms of the vain-gods,
Whose images exceeded those of Damascus and Samaria,
Shall I not, as I have done to Samaria and to her vain-gods,
So do to Jerusalem and her images?"
And it shall be that when *the* Lord has completed all his work,
In mount Zion and in Jerusalem,
I will visit upon *the* fruit of *the* proud heart of *the* king of Assyria,
And upon *the* vain glory of *the* loftiness of his eyes.
"For saith he, "By strength of mine hand have I done *it*,
And by my wisdom, for I am discerning;
And I have removed boundaries of peoples,
And their treasures have I plundered,
And like a hero, I brought down *the* enthroned,
And my hand lighted on *the* riches of the peoples as on a nest;
And as one gathers forsaken eggs,
So have I gathered all the earth,
And none was there that moved wing,
Opened mouth or chirped."

Chapter X. 15—22.

Is the axe to vaunt itself against him who hews with it?
Is the saw to boast itself against him who wields it?
As if a rod could wield Him who lifts it!
As if a staff could lift H*im who is* not wood!
Therefore the Lord, Adonai Sabaoth,
Will send leanness on his lusty ones,
And under his glory kindle a kindling
Like *the* kindling of a fire.
And *the* light of Israel shall be for a fire,
And his Holy One for a flame,
And it burns and devours his thorns,
And his thistles in a single day,
And *the* glory of his forest and fruitful field,
It will consume, both soul and body;
And it is as when a sick man wastes away.*
And *the* remnant of his forest trees shall be scanty,
So that a child may note them down.
And in that day it comes to pass,
That the remnant of Israel and *the* escaped of *the* house of Jacob.
Shall lean no more on him that smote them,
But lean upon Yahveh, the Holy One of Israel, in truth.
A REMNANT-SHALL-RETURN, a remnant of Jacob,
To El *the* mighty:
For though thy people, O Israel, were like sand of the sea,
Only A REMNANT-SHALL-RETURN of them:
A desolation is decreed, bringing in justice like a flood;

CHAPTER X. 23—32

For desolation and doom doth Adonai Yahveh Sabaoth
  execute within all the land.
Thus therefore saith Adonai Yahveh Sabaoth,
Fear not, O my people who dwellest in Zion, because of
  Assur, *if* with staff he smite thee,
And lift up his rod against thee, in *the* manner of Egypt;
For yet a very little while, and *my* indignation is
  completed,
And my anger, for their destruction.
And Yahveh Sabaoth brandishes a scourge over him,
As *at the* smiting of Midian at *the* rock of Oreb;
And *as* his rod was over the sea,
So he lifts it up as in *the* manner of Egypt.
And it comes to pass in that day,
That his burden removes from thy shoulder,
And his yoke from off thy neck,
And by fatness is a yoke broken.

He is come upon Aiath—he passes through Migron;
At Michmash he lays up his baggage:
They go through the pass,
Geba is their quarters,
Ramah trembles,
Gibeah of Saul flies!
Daughter of Gallim lift up thy voice;
Listen Laishah—answer her Anathoth.*
Madmenah wanders away;
The inhabitants of Gebim save *their goods* by flight.
Yet *for* the day he halts at Nob:
He shakes his hand at *the* mount of Zion's daughter,

Chapter X. 32—XI. 7.

The hill of Jerusalem!
But see! the Lord Yahveh Sabaoth,
Lops a crowning-branch with terrific crash,
And *the* tall of stature are cut down,
And the haughty are brought low,
And with iron he fells *the* thickets of the forest,
And the Lebanon falls by a Majestic One.
Then a shoot comes forth from *the* stem of Jesse,
And a scion from his roots bears fruit;
And *the* spirit of Yahveh rests upon him,
A spirit of wisdom and of discernment,
A spirit of counsel and of might,
A spirit of knowledge and of reverence for Yahveh,
And he finds a sweet savour in reverence for Yahveh;
And not at *the* sight of his eyes will he judge,
Nor by *the* hearing of his ears will he decide,
But judges *the* poor with fairness,
And decides with equity for *the* meek of *the* land,
And smites *the* land with rod of his mouth,
And with breath of his lips will slay *the* wicked :
And justice is *the* girdle of his loins,
And faithfulness *the* girdle of his reins.

Then wolf lodges with lamb,
And leopard will lie down with kid,
And calf and young lion and fatling together—
And a little child is leading them.
And heifer and she-bear will feed together.
Together will their young lie down,
And a lion eat straw like an ox;

Chapter XI. 8—14.

And a suckling plays at hole of asp,
And weaned-child reaches forth its hand to den of basilisk :
They will not harm nor destroy in all my holy mountain,
For the land is full of knowledge of Yahveh,
As waters which cover *the* sea.

Also it comes to pass in that day—
A root of Jesse which stands for an ensign to peoples—
To it nations will repair,
And its resting-place becomes a glory.
And in that day it comes to pass,
Adonai will again the second time put forth his hand
To recover the remnant of his people that shall be left
From Asshur and from Egypt,
And from Pathros and from Cush and from Elam,
And from Shinar and from Hamath and from coasts of the sea ;
And he rears an ensign to *the* nations
And gathers *the* outcasts of Israel,
And will collect *the* dispersed of Judah,
From *the* four corners of the earth ;
And *the* jealousy of Ephraim departs,
And *the* adversaries of Judah shall be cut off ;
Ephraim will not be jealous of Judah,
And Jacob will not vex Ephraim ;
But they fly upon *the* shoulder of the Philistines westward ;
Together they will spoil the sons of *the* east
And they lay their hands on Edom and Moab,

Chapter XI. 14—XII. 6.

And *the* sons of Ammon obey them.
Then Yahveh devotes *to dryness the* tongue of *the* Egyptian sea,
And shakes his hand over the river with violence of his blast,
And strikes it into seven channels
And makes men cross it dryshod ;
And a highway is made for *the* remnant of his people which shall be left, from Assyria,
As there was made for Israel in *the* day of his coming up from *the* land of Egypt.

And in that day thou sayest
' I will praise thee, Yahveh, for *though* thou wast wrath with me,
' Thy wrath has turned away and Thou hast comforted me.
' Behold, El is my deliverance !
' I will trust and not be afraid,
' For my strength and my song is Yah-Yahveh,
' And He has become my deliverance.'
And with joy ye draw waters
From fountains of the deliverance.
And ye say in that day,
' Praise Yahveh, invoke his name ;
' Declare his deeds among *the* peoples,
' Record it that his name is exalted.
' Sing ye *to* Yahveh for he has done excellent things ;
' Known is this in all the earth,
' Cry out and shout, inhabitress of Zion,
' For great in thy midst is *the* Holy One of Israel.'

CHAPTERS XIII. XIV., 1—23.

CHAPTER XIII. 1—9.

Summons to the Medes, and the downfall of Babylon.

Oracle of Babylon, which Isaiah *the* son of Amoz saw.

On a bare mountain raise ye a banner,
Uplift a cry to them, wave *the* hand,
That they may enter *the* gates of *the* princes.
I give a charge to my consecrated ones,
My mighty ones I also call for my wrath,
My proudly exulting ones.

A noise of a tumult on *the* mountains as of much people!
A noise of an uproar of kingdoms, of assembled nations!
Yahveh Sabaoth is mustering a host *for* battle!
They are coming from a far-off land,
From *the* end of the Heavens,
Yahveh and instruments of his wrath,
To lay waste all the earth!
Wail ye! for Yahveh's day is near,
As a destruction from *the* Mighty One will it come!*
Therefore all hands shall hang down,
And every heart of man will melt:
They are terrified; pangs and throes shall seize on them;
They shall writhe like a woman in travail,
Each shall look with amazement at his neighbour,
—Faces of flame their faces!

Behold, a day of Yahveh comes,
Cruel, and wrath, and a glow of anger,

Chapter XIII. 9—18.

To make the earth a desolation,
And it will destroy its sinners out of it :
For *the* stars of the Heavens and their Orions
Shall not give forth their light ;
The sun is darkened in his going forth,
And *the* moon will not suffer her light to shine.
And I visit upon *the* world *its* evil,
And their iniquities upon *the* wicked,
And I still *the* arrogance of *the* proud,
And *the* haughtiness of terrible ones will I abase :
I will make men more scarce than gold,
And a man than Ophir's gold-wedge.
Wherefore I will cause the heavens to tremble,
And the earth shall move, quaking from its place
At *the* wrath of Yahveh Sabaoth,
And at *the* day of *the* glow of his anger.
And it is as with a chased roe,
And like sheep which no man folds,
They shall turn each towards his own people,
And flee every one to his own land.
Every one who is found shall be thrust through,
And every one who is caught shall fall by *the* sword,
And their infants shall be dashed down before their eyes,
Their houses plundered, and their wives ravished.

Behold I stir up the Medes against them,
Who make no account of silver,
And as for gold, have no pleasure in it.
And bows shall dash youths in pieces,
And on fruit of womb they will have no compassion,

Chapter XIII. 18—22.

Their eye will not spare children.
And Babylon, glory of kingdoms,
Proud ornament of Chaldeans,
Becomes as when Elohim overthrew Sodom and Gomorrah ;
It will not be inhabited for ever,
Nor dwelt in for generation and generation ;
And Arab will not pitch tent there,
And shepherds will not cause *their flocks* to lie down there ;
But beasts of the desert lie there,
And owlets fill their houses,
And ostriches dwell there,
And satyrs will dance there ;
And in the palaces thereof wolves howl to one another,
And jackals in *the* mansions of luxury.
Her time is nearly come,
And her days shall not be prolonged.

CHAPTER XIV. 1, 2.

But Yahveh will have compassion on Jacob,
And again chooses Israel,
And gives them rest in their own land,
And the alien is joined to them ;
And they cleave to *the* house of Jacob,—
And heathen take them, and bring them to their place,
And *the* house of Israel takes them in possession,
In *the* land of Yahveh, for servants and for handmaids ;

Chapter XIV. 2—10.

And they capture their captors, and rule over their oppressors.

And it comes to pass in *the* day that Yahveh gives thee rest
From thy distress, and from thy disquiet,
And from the hard servitude which men laid upon thee,
Then dost thou take up this strain of derision
Against *the* king of Babylon, and sayest :
How stilled *the* tyrant ! *how* stilled *his* oppression !
The staff of *the* wicked, *the* sceptre of tyrants, has Yahveh broken,
Which in wrath smote peoples with ceaseless smiting,
Trampling on nations in wrath, a trampling without restraint !
The whole earth is at rest, is still : they break out into shouting :
The cypresses. also rejoice at thee, *the* cedars of Lebanon, saying,
' Since thou liest low, no feller will come up against us.'

Sheol beneath is stirred because of thee, to meet thy arrival,
It arouses *the* shades for thee, all *who were* leaders on earth,
It makes all kings of nations to arise from their thrones.
They all answer and say to thee,
' Thou too art become weak as we, Thou art become like us :

THE PROPHECIES OF ISAIAH. 37

CHAPTER XIV. 11—19.

'Thy pride is brought down to Sheol, the sound of thy lyres :
'Beneath thee is spread corruption, and worms are thy covering !'

How art thou fallen from heaven, Bright one, son of *the* Dayspring !
Felled thou art to *the* ground, who didst overpower nations !
And thou saidst in thine heart, I will mount the heavens,
To *the* stars of El will I exalt my throne,
And take my seat in *the* mount of assembly, in *the* recesses of *the* north ;
I will mount above heights of clouds—will be like *the* Most High.
Surely thou art brought down to Sheol, to *the* recesses of *the* pit.

They who see thee, gaze *and* mark *thee* well, and say,
'Is this the man who made the earth to tremble, who made kingdoms quake ;
'Made *the* world as a wilderness, and laid its cities to waste,
'Released not his captives for their home ?
'All kings of nations, all of them lie in honour, each in his house,
'But thou from thy grave art flung away like a loathed branch,
'Clad with sword-pierced slain, like a trampled carcass.

Chapter XIV. 20—23.

' They who go down to *the* stones of *the* pit—
' Not with them art thou joined in burial ;
' Because thou hast destroyed thy land, hast slain thy people."
Unnamed for ever *shall be the* seed of evildoers !
Prepare a slaughter for his children, for their fathers' sin,
Lest they arise and possess *the* earth
And fill *the* face of *the* world with ruins.

And I arise against them—*it is* an utterance of Yahveh Sabaoth,—
And I cut off from Babylon name and remnant,
And seed and progeny—an utterance of Yahveh ;—
And I make it *the* possession of bittern, and pools of waters,
And I sweep it with sweeping-broom of destruction :
—an utterance of Yahveh Sabaoth.

CHAPTER XIV. 24—26.

Downfall of Assyria. A Fragment, probably misplaced.

Yahveh Sabaoth has sworn, saying,
Surely as I have purposed, so shall it be,
And as I have counselled, that shall stand ;
To crush Assyria in my land,
And on my mountains will I tread him down :
And his yoke removes from them,
And his burden will remove from his shoulder.
This is the purpose which is purposed for the whole earth,

THE PROPHECIES OF ISAIAH.

CHAPTER XIV. 26, 27.

And this the hand that is outstretched over all nations.
For Yahveh Sabaoth has purposed,
And who may disannul it?
And his hand *is* the outstretched,
And who may turn it back?

CHAPTER XIV. 28—32.

Philistia must beware of rejoicing in the judgment thus announced (in xiv. 24—27*).*

In *the* year King Ahaz died was this oracle:
Rejoice not, Philistia, all of thee,
That a rod which smote thee is broken;
For from *the* snake's root springs forth a basilisk,
And its fruit, a winged serpent!
And *the* first-born of *the* poor feed,
And the needy shall lie down in security,
But thy root I kill with drought—
And thy remnant shall he slay.
Howl, gate! cry aloud, city;
O Philistia, thou art all of thee dissolved *with fear:*
For from *the* north comes forth a smoke,
And none walks singly in their troops—
And what shall one answer *the* messengers of *the* nations?
'That Yahveh has founded Zion,
And in her the afflicted of his people will confide.'

CHAPTERS XV. XVI.

CHAPTER XV. 1—6.

A Prophecy against Moab, whose king had revolted. A claim of Tribute, xvi. 1. *(Comp.* 2 *Kings* iii. 4, *&c.) Denunciations of Moab's pride and idolatry.*

The oracle of Moab;

  For in a night is Ar-Moab laid waste *and* ruined!
  For in a night is Kir-Moab laid waste, ruined!
  He is gone up to the temple and Dibon, the high places, to weep;
  On Nebo and on Medeba shall Moab wail,
  On all their heads baldness,
  Every head shorn.
  In his streets they gird on sackcloth,
  On its roofs and in its open places every one will wail,
  Flowing down with tears:
  And Heshbon cries aloud, and Elealeh;
  Even to Jahaz their voice is heard;
  Therefore *the* warriors of Moab shall cry aloud,
  His soul shall quail within him. *
  My heart cries out for Moab;
  His fugitives *wander* to Zoar *like* a heifer of three years old:
  For the ascent to the Luhith—with weeping shall he ascend it, *
  For, *in the* way of Horonaim shall they raise a cry of destruction,
  For, *the* waters of Nimrim shall be desolate,

THE PROPHECIES OF ISAIAH. 41

CHAPTERS XV. 6—9. XVI. 1—5.

For grass is dried up—herbage consumed—
There is nothing green.
Therefore *the* abundance they have gotten, and their store—
Over *the* torrent of the willows shall they remove them ;
For the cry encircles the border of Moab,
Her wail *reaches* to Eglaim,
Even *to* Beer-Elim her wail :
For, the waters of Dimon are full of blood ; *
For, fresh *evils* will I bring on Dimon,
Unto *the* escaped of Moab, a lion,
And unto *the* remnant of *the* land.

' Send ye *the* lambs of *the* ruler of *the* land.
' From Sela towards *the* desert,
' To *the* Mount of Sion's daughter.'
Then comes it to pass that like a wandering bird driven *from* nest,
Shall be *the* daughters of Moab *at the* fords of Arnon :
' Propose advice, *say they*—' come to a decision—
' Make thy shadow like night in mid-noontide :
' Shelter outcasts : betray not a fugitive :
' Let Moab's outcasts sojourn with thee,
' Be thou a shelter to them from *the* face of *the* spoiler ;
' For *the* oppressor is no more, destruction is finished,
' He who trampled down has vanished out of the land,
' And by kindness has a throne been established,
' And one sits upon it with faithfulness in David's tent,
' Judging and seeking justice and speeding right.'

Chapter XVI. 6—13.

We have heard of *the* pride of Moab, *the* very proud,
His haughtiness and his arrogance and his wrath,
The falseness of his boastings—
Therefore shall Moab wail for Moab, wail entirely,
For *the* ruins of Kir-Hareseth shall ye moan, *the* smitten utterly.
For the fields of Heshbon shall languish;
The vine of Sibmah—
Lords of nations have struck down its choice plants;—
They reached to Yaser, strayed to *the* desert,
Her shoots spread forth, passed beyond the sea.
Therefore will I weep with weeping of Yazer for Sibmah's vine;
With my tears will I water thee,- O Heshbon and Elealeh,
For on thy summer-fruits and on thy vintage has a war-cry fallen,
And joy and gladness is taken from the fruitful field,
And in *the* vineyards they sing not, they shout not.
And in *the* presses no treader treads out *the* wine—
The vintage-cry have I made to cease.
Therefore my bowels shall sound like a harp for Moab,
And my inward parts for Kir-Hareseth.
Then comes it to pass that when Moab appears,
When he wearies himself on the high place,
And comes to his sanctuary to pray, that he shall not prevail.

This is the word which Yahveh long since spoke concerning Moab:

Chapter XVI. 13, 14.

But now Yahveh speaks, saying :
Within three years as *the* years of an hireling,
And Moab's glory shall be abased,
With all the great multitude,
And *the* remnant *shall be* very small, without power.

CHAPTER XVII. 1—6.

The Oracle of Damascus.
See! Damascus is removed from being a city,
And is become a heap, a ruin. *
Forsaken *are the* cities of Aroer, *
They are *given up* to flocks,
And they lie down, and there is none to alarm ;
And stronghold ceases from Ephraim,
And kingdom from Damascus, and *the* remnant of
    Aram ;—
They become like *the* glory of *the* sons of Israel :
—An utterance of Yahveh Sabaoth.

And in that day it comes to pass,
That Jacob's glory will be wasted,
And *the* fatness of his flesh grow lean :
And it is as when a reaper gathers standing corn,
And his arm will reap *the* ears—
Yea, it is as when one harvests ears in *the* valley of
    Rephaim,
And gleanings only are left in it,
As in *the* beating of an olive tree,
Two, three berries on a highest bough-top,

Chapter XVII. 6—11.

Four, five, on *the* branches of *the* fruit-tree.
An utterance of Yahveh *the* Elohim of Israel.

In that day shall the earth-born have regard to his maker,
And his eye shall look to Israel's Holy One;
But the altars—work of his own hands—he will not regard,
Nor look on that which his own fingers have made
The Ashéras and the sun-images.
In that day his strong cities
Become like deserted places of forest and hill-top,
Which *men* deserted before *the* children of Israel,
And it shall become a desolation.
For thou didst forget *the* Elohim of thy safety,
And *the* rock of thy strength didst not remember;
Therefore thou plantedst delightsome plants
And didst set foreign scions —
In *the* day thou plantedst it thou didst hedge *it* in,
And at morn thou didst make thy scion blossom;
But fled is *the* harvest in *the* day of possession,
And grievous *is the* sorrow.

CHAPTERS XVII. 12—14.—XVIII.

Chapter XVII. 12—14.

Destruction of the Assyrian forces—specially announced to Æthiopia (Cush) as in alliance, or sympathy, with Israel.

Hah! a tumult of many peoples!
Like a tumult of seas shall they be tumultuous!

THE PROPHECIES OF ISAIAH. 45

CHAPTER XVII. 12—14. XVIII. 1—5.

And a roar of nations—
Nations—like a roaring of mighty waters shall they roar !
But He rebukes it, and it flies afar,
And is chased like chaff of mountains before a blast,
And like whirling dust before an hurricane.
At eventide, behold terror ;
Ere morning, it is gone !
This *the* portion of those who spoil us,
And *the* lot of those who plunder us.

Hah ! land of rustling wings,
Which art beyond *the* rivers of Cush ;
Which sendest ambassadors by sea,
And in vessels of papyrus on face of waters !
Go, ye light messengers,
To a nation robust and fierce,
To a people terrible from the first, and hitherto,
To a nation of domineering and trampling down,
Whose land rivers divide.
All ye inhabitants of *the* world
And dwellers on earth,
At *the* lifting of a signal *on the* mountains, behold,
And when a trumpet is sounded, hearken.

For thus saith Yahveh to me :
In my dwelling place will I keep me still and look on,
Like clear heat in sunshine,
Like dew-cloud in heat of harvest :
But before harvest, when blossom is over,
And a bud is become a ripening grape,

Chapter XVIII. 5—7.

Then with pruning-hooks he lops the branches,
And the tendrils he takes away *and* cuts off:
To mountain bird of prey they shall be left together,
And to beast of the land;
And the bird of prey shall summer upon them,
And every beast of the land shall winter upon them.
At that time shall a gift be brought to Yahveh Sabaoth,
From a nation robust and fierce,
And from a people terrible from the first, and hitherto,
A nation of domineering and down-trampling,
Whose land rivers divide,
To *the* place of *the* house Yahveh Sabaoth, Zion's hill.

CHAPTER XIX. 1—4.

Oracle of Egypt.

See! Yahveh riding on a swift cloud—
And to Egypt he comes!
And at his presence the vain-gods of Egypt shake,
And Egypt's heart will melt within it.
And I spur on Egyptians against Egyptians,
And they fight each against his brother,
And each against his fellow;
City against city, kingdom against kingdom,
And Egypt's spirit is made empty within it,
And its counsel will I destroy;
And they resort to the vain-gods and the whisperers,
And the necromancers and the wizards.
And I shut up the Egyptians into *the* hand of a hard Lord,

THE PROPHECIES OF ISAIAH. 47

Chapter XIX. 4—13.

And a fierce king shall rule over them.
—The utterance of the Lord, Yahveh Sabaoth.
And waters fail from the sea,
And *the* River is wasted and dry ;
And rivers become putrid,
And *the* streams of Egypt are wasted and dried up :
Reed and flag wither,
The meadows by *the Nile*-stream, at *the* stream-mouth,
And all that is sown by *the* stream,
Dries up, is scattered, and is no more,
And the fishermen sigh,
And all who cast hook into *the* stream lament,
And they who spread nets on *the* face of *the* waters
 languish :
And they who dress *the* carded flax are ashamed,
They too who weave white linen !
And her pillars are become broken down,
And all who work for hire are sad of soul.

Surely, foolish are Zoan's nobles,
The wise men of Pharaoh's counsellors—brutish *their*
 counsel !
How say ye to Pharaoh, 'a son of sages am I, a son of
 ancient kings ?'
Where *are* they then, thy sages ?—
And let them now announce to thee, and let them know,
What Yahveh Sabaoth has counselled concerning Egypt.
The princes of Zoan are become foolish,
Deceived are *the* princes of Noph,

Chapter XIX. 13—21.

And they have led Egypt astray
Who are the corner stone of her tribes.
Yahveh has mingled within her a spirit of giddiness,
So that they have made Egypt to reel in all his work,
Like *the* reeling of drunkard in his vomit.
Nor shall there be any work for Egypt,
Which head or tail, palm branch or bulrush, may work.

In that day Egypt shall be like women,
And it trembles and quakes,
At *the* shaking of Yahveh Sabaoth's hand,
Which He shakes over it.
And the land of Judah becomes a terror to Egypt:
Whoever mentions it to him shudders,
Because of *the* purpose of Yahveh Sabaoth,
Which He purposes against it.
In that day shall be five cities in *the* land of Egypt
Speaking *the* language of Canaan,
And swearing to Yahveh Sabaoth;
One shall be called "City of the Sun."
In that day shall be an altar to Yahveh
In *the* midst of *the* land of Egypt,
And near its boundary a pillar to Yahveh;
And it becomes a sign and a witness,
For Yahveh Sabaoth in *the* land of Egypt;
When they shall cry to Yahveh because of oppressors,
And He will send them a deliverer and a champion,
And will rescue them.
And Yahveh becomes known to Egypt,

CHAPTER XIX. 21—25.

And Egyptians know Yahveh in that day,
And serve with sacrifice and oblation,
And vow a vow unto Yahveh and pay it.
So Yahveh smites Egypt, smiting and healing,
And they turn unto Yahveh,
And he is entreated of them and heals them.
In that day there shall be a highway from Egypt towards Assyria,
So that Assyria comes into Egypt and Egypt into Assyria,
And Egyptians serve with the Assyrians.

In that day Israel shall be a third to Egypt and to Assyria,
A Blessing in *the* midst of the earth,
Wherewith Yahveh Sabaoth has blessed him, saying,
Blessed be my people Egypt,
And Assyria, work of my hands,
And Israel my inheritance.

CHAPTER XX. 1, 2.

Isaiah, by a symbolical action, sets forth the fate of those in whom Egypt and Palestine trusted.

In *the* year when Tartan came to Ashdod, when sent by Sargon king of Assyria, and fought against Ashdod and took it—at that time Yahveh spake by Isaiah son of Amoz, saying:

Chapter XX. 2—6.

Go and loose the sackcloth from off thy loins
And unbind thy sandals from off thy foot.
 And he did so, walking naked and barefoot: Then Yahveh said,
  As my servant Isaiah has walked naked and barefoot,
   for three years a sign
And a portent against Egypt and against Cush,
So shall *the* King of Assyria lead the captivity of Egypt,
And the exiles of Cush, young and old,
Naked and barefoot and their hind-parts uncovered,
A disgrace to Egypt.
Then are they afraid and ashamed
Of Cush their confidence and of Egypt their ornament.
In that day dwellers in this coast say,
' Lo, such is our trust to which we fled for succour,
' To be delivered from *the* king of Assyria,
' And how shall WE escape ? '

CHAPTER XXI. 1, 2.

The destruction of the "WILDERNESS BY THE SEA," *i.e., Babylon on the Euphrates, by Medes and Persians.*

An oracle concerning *the* wilderness by the sea.
 Like hurricanes in *the* south driving past
 It comes from *the* wilderness, from a terrible land.
 A grievous vision is revealed to me,
 The plunderer plundering and the destroyer destroying:—
 Go up, Elam : besiege, Media—

Chapter XXI. 2—10.

All sighing I make to cease.

Therefore are my loins filled with anguish;
Throes seize me like *the* throes of her who travails—
I writhe so that I cannot hear,
I am so troubled that I cannot see;
My heart is bewildered—alarms dismay me.
He hath made the evening of my pleasure a terror to me.
A setting out the table—a watching the watch—Eating, drinking!
'Up ye princes, anoint *the* shield.'

For thus saith Adonai to me:
Go station a watchman—
What he shall see let him report.
And he saw riders, horsemen in double rank,
Riders on asses, riders on camels:
And he gave heed with utmost heed.
Then he cried out *like* a lion,
'My Lord, I stand on *the* watch-tower all day long,
'And all the nights am I posted in my ward:
'And lo! there come men riding, horsemen in double rank,'
And he cried aloud and said, 'Fallen, fallen is Babylon,
'And all *the* images of her gods hath he broken against *the* ground.'
O my threshed one and son of my winnowing-floor!
What I have heard from Yahveh Sabaoth, Israel's Elohim, have I proclaimed to you.

CHAPTER XXI. 11, 12.

The oracle concerning Dumah (an abbreviated form of Edom), with implied allusion to the silence (Dumah) of desolation.

Oracle of Dumah.
Out of Seir one cries to me,
'Watchman! what *time* of *the* night?
'Watchman! what *time* of *the* night?"
The watchman answers,
'Morning comes and also night!'
If ye will enquire, enquire:
Turn, come.

CHAPTER XXI. 13—16.

The Oracle "IN THE EVENING," *against the Dedanites, and other Arabian Tribes.*

In thickets must ye lodge in *the* evening*
Ye caravans of Dedanites!
Ye inhabitants of *the* land of Tema,
Bring forth water to meet *the* thirsty,
Be ready with his bread for *the* fugitive;
For from *the* face of swords do they flee,
From *the* face of drawn sword,
And before bended bow,
And before *the* press of war.
For thus said Yahveh to me:
Within yet a year according to a hireling's years
And all *the* glory of Kedar is at an end;
And *the* number of bows that is left

CHAPTER XXI. 16.
Of Kedar's mighty sons, shall be minished,
For Yahveh, *the* Elohim of Israel, has spoken.

CHAPTER XXII. 1—6.
With reference to judgments upon Jerusalem.
Oracle of ' a valley of vision.'
What ails thee then, that ye have all mounted *the* roofs—
Thou that art full of uproar, tumultuous city, joyous town !
Thy slain are not *the* slain of sword
Nor *the* dead of battle !

All thy chieftains have fled together :
By *the* archers are they taken prisoners ;
All that are found of thee are made prisoners together,
Who had fled afar.

Therefore, say I, ' Look away from me—I would weep bitterly—
' Strive not to comfort me
' For *the* spoiling of *the* daughter of my people.'
For a day of tumult and of treading down and of confusion*
Hath Adonai Yahveh Sabaoth, in ' a valley of vision,'
Unwalling the wall,*
And a cry *reaches* the mount.
And Elam carries the quiver,
With chariots, men, horsemen,
And Kir makes bare *the* shield,

Chapter XXII. 7—14.

And thy choicest vallies are filled with chariots,
And the horsemen post themselves gate-ward,
And He will draw aside the veil of Judah.

But thou lookest in that day to *the* armour of *the* forest-house,
And ye see that *the* breaches of David's city are many,
And ye collect the waters of the lower pool,
And the houses of Jerusalem ye number,
And ye break down the houses to fortify the wall,
And ye make a reservoir between the two walls
For waters of the old conduit:
But, Him who made it ye regard not,
And to Him that fashioned it of old ye look not.
And in that day Adonai Yahveh Sabaoth will summon to weeping and to wailing
And to baldness and to girding with sackcloth;
But behold, joy and gladness,
Killing oxen and slaughtering sheep,
Eating flesh and drinking wine :—
'Eat and drink, for we die to morrow.'
Therefore in mine ears is it revealed by Yahveh Sabaoth,
This iniquity shall not be forgiven you till ye die,
Saith Adonai Yahveh Sabaoth.

CHAPTER XXII. 15.

The removal of Shebna from office at Court. The advancement of Eliakim.

Thus saith Adonai Yahveh Sabaoth:

THE PROPHECIES OF ISAIAH.

CHAPTER XXII. 15—24.

Go, get thee to this minister,
To Shebna who is over the house, *and say*,
What hast thou here, and whom hast thou here,
That thou hewest thee out a sepulchre here,
Hewing out his sepulchre on high,
Cutting out an abiding-place for himself in *the* rock !
Lo, with strong cast Yahveh casts thee out—
Wrapping He wraps thee up,
And rolling He will roll thee *as* a roll,
Like a ball into a spacious land :
There shalt thou die,
And there *shall be* thy splendid chariots,
Thou shame of thy master's house !
And I thrust thee from thy station,
And from thy place He pulls thee down.
And it comes to pass in that day,
That I summon my servant,
Eliakim, son of Hilkiah,
And with thy robe I invest him,
And will bind him with thy girdle,
And into his hand will I commit thy government :
And he becomes a Father to *the* inhabitants of Jerusalem,
And to *the* house of Judah.
And I lay upon his shoulder *the* key of David's house,
So that he opens and no man shuts,
And shuts and no man opens :
And as a nail in a sure place I fasten him,
And he becomes a seat of honour to his father's house,
And on him they hang all *the* honour of his Father's house,

CHAPTER XXII. 24, 25.

The scions and the offshoots,
All the small vessels, from vessels of the cups even to all the flagon-like vessels.

In that day—an utterance of Yahveh Sabaoth—
The nail fastened in a sure place gives way,
And it is cut down and falls,
And the burden that was upon it is cut down :
For Yahveh has spoken.

CHAPTER XXIII. 1—4.

The fall of Tyre by means of Assyria, which under Sargon had conquered Babylonia. For seventy years (i.e., a long time) Tyre shall remain unchanged as if under a single reign, and then recover her prosperity.

Oracle of Tyre.
Wail, ships of Tarshish,
For she is spoiled of house, of access!
From *the* land of Chittim it is disclosed to them.

Be silent, ye inhabitants of *the* coast,
Which sea-traversing merchants of Zidon did crowd :
And on great waters was *the* grain of Shihor,
The harvest of *the* River was her revenue,
So that she became a mart of nations!

Be ashamed, Zidon, for *the* sea speaks,
The fortress of the sea, saying,
' I have not travailed nor brought forth,

THE PROPHECIES OF ISAIAH. 57

CHAPTER XXIII. 4—13.

'' I have not reared youths, nor brought up virgins.'
When *the* tidings reach Egypt,
At *the* tidings of Tyre shall they be pained.

Pass over to Tarshish,
Howl, inhabitants of *the* coast !
Is this your exulting city,
Whose ancientness is of ancient days ?
Her own feet carry her far away to sojourn !
Who has purposed this
Against Tyre the bestower of crowns,
Whose merchants were princes,
Whose traders *the* honoured of earth ?
Yahveh Sabaoth purposed it,
To profane *the* pride of all splendour,
To debase all *the* honoured of earth.

Overflow thy land like *the* River ;
O daughter of Tarshish, there is no more restraint ;
He stretched out His hand over the sea,
Kingdoms has He made to tremble—
Concerning Canaan has Yahveh commanded
To destroy her fortresses.
And he said, Exult no more,
Violated Virgin, daughter of Sidon—
Arise, pass over to Chittim—
Even there thou shalt not rest
Behold *the* land of the Chaldees—
This people is no more ;
Assyria has made it over to beasts of the desert ;

Chapter XXIII. 13—18.

They raised their *siege*-towers,
They overthrew her palaces,
He has made her a ruin.
Wail, ships of Tarshish,
For your stronghold is destroyed!

And it comes to pass in that day,
That Tyre is forgotten seventy years,
As *the* days of a single king :
But at *the* end of seventy years it shall be with Tyre
As in a harlot's song ;
' Take *thy* harp, go round *the* city, forgotten harlot !
' Touch the strings skilfully ; sing many a song,
' That thou mayest be remembered.'
And it comes to pass at *the* end of seventy years,
Yahveh will visit Tyre,
And she returns to her hire,
And fornicates with all kingdoms of the earth,
That are on *the* face of the world,
But her merchandize and her hire become holy to Yahveh;
It shall not be treasured up nor kept in store,
But her merchandise shall be for them that dwell before Yahveh
For abundant food, and for splendid vestments.

THE PROPHECIES OF ISAIAH.

CHAPTERS XXIV. XXVII.

CHAPTER XXIV. 1—7.

The desolation of the land: the return of the Jews from exile: Hymns to be sung by the Prophet in the name of the people, and by the people themselves: the destruction of Babylon: the restoration of the Theocracy.

See! Yahveh pours out the land and empties it *
And turns its face upside down
And scatters its inhabitants!
And it comes to pass that as people, so priest;
As servant, so his master;
As maid, so her mistress;
As buyer, so seller:
As lender, so borrower;
As debtor, so creditor;—
With emptying emptied, with spoiling spoiled is *the* land,*
For this word has Yahveh spoken.

The land wails, fails ;*
The world fades, fails;
The loftiness of *the* people of the land languishes,
And the earth is polluted under its inhabitants;
For they have transgressed precepts, violated law,
Broken an everlasting covenant.
Therefore a curse devours *the* land,
And *the* dwellers therein are punished for guilt;
Therefore *the* dwellers on *the* land are burned up,
And few are left.
The new wine mourns, *the* vine languishes,

Chapter XXIV. 7—17.

All that were glad of heart are sighing!
Ceased is *the* mirth of timbrels,
Ended *the* uproar of *the* joyous,
Ceased is *the* mirth of harp.
They shall not drink wine with song,
Bitter to them that quaff it shall be strong drink;
A city of desolation *is* broken down,
Closed every house from entry;
In *the* streets is a cry because of the wine.
All joy has set,
The mirth of the land is banished,
Desolation is left in *the* city,
And *the* gate is smitten *into* ruins.
For so shall it be within the land amid the peoples,
As when an olive tree is beaten,
As a gleaning when *the* vintage is done:
These shall uplift their voice;
Shall shout for *the* majesty of Yahveh,
From *the* sea they cry aloud;—
'Wherefore in *the* countries glorify Yahveh,
'In *the* countries of the sea, *the* name of Yahveh, Elohim of Israel!
From *the* outskirts of the land we hear songs,
'Honour for *the* righteous!'
But I said, 'For me is pining—for me is pining! Alas for me!'
The spoilers spoil,
And spoilers spoil *the* spoil
A scaring, and pit-snare and snare*
Are upon thee, O inhabitant of the land!

CHAPTER XXIV. 18—23.—XXV. 1, 2.

And it is so that one who flies from sound of the scaring
Will fall into the pit-snare ;
And one who comes up from *the* midst of the pit-snare,
Will be taken in *the* snare ;
For lattices from on high have opened,
And *the* foundations of the land tremble.
Quaking the land quakes !*
Breaking, *the* land breaks up !
Shaking, *the* land shakes !
Reeling, *the* land reels like a drunkard,
And rocks to and fro like a hammock !
And her rebellion lies heavy on her,
And she falls and rises not again.

And it comes to pass in that day that Yahveh will visit
    the Host of the Height in *the* height,
And kings of the Earth on the Earth.
And they are gathered with gathering of prisoners for
    the pit,*
And in prison are imprisoned,
And after many days shall they be visited *in mercy ;*
And the moon blushes and the sun is ashamed,
When Yahveh Sabaoth reigns
On Mount Sion and in Jerusalem,—
And before his ancients, *in* glory.
Yahveh ! thou art my Elohim ;
Thee will I exalt, will praise thy name ;
For thou hast wrought out a wonder,—
Counsels long since *purposed*—truth, faithfulness !
Thou hast made of a city an heap,

Chapter XXV. 2—9.

A fenced town into a ruin,
A fortress of aliens to be no city, —
Never shall it be rebuilt.
Therefore shall peoples of might honour thee,
Cities of terrible nations shall fear thee ;
For to *the* weak thou hast become a stronghold,
A stronghold to *the* needy in his strait,
From storm a shelter, from heat a shade ;
For *the* blast of *the* terrible *was* like a storm *against* a wall.
As heat on a parched land,
Didst thou subdue *the* uproar of *the* alien ;
*A*s heat by shadow of a cloud,
The song of *the* terrible ones is humbled.

And Yahveh Sabaoth makes in this mountain for all the peoples
A Feast of fat things, a feast of vat-kept wine,*
Of marrowy fat things, of vat-kept wine refined.
And in this mountain He swallows up
The face of the veil which veils all the peoples,
And the covering that covers all the nations ;
He swallows up death for ever,
And from all faces Adonai Yahveh wipes away tears,
And takes away from off all the earth *the* reproach of his people,
For Yahveh has spoken.
In that day it is said, ' Lo, our Elohim,
' For whom we waited that He should deliver us !
' This is Yahveh for whom we waited,

CHAPTER XXV. 9--12. XXVI. 1—8.

'Let us rejoice and be glad in his deliverance.'
For on this mountain *the* hand of Yahveh rests,
And in his own place is Moab trodden down,
As straw is trodden down in water of a dunghill:
And *though* he spread forth his hand in its midst,
As the swimmer spreads *them* forth to swim,
Yet He brings down his pride,
Together with *the* manœuvres of his hands;
And *the* fortress of thy lofty walls He throws down,
Lays low, levels with *the* ground, even to *the* dust.

In that day will this song be sung in Judah's land:
'A city of strength is ours,
'For walls and bulwark He appoints deliverance:
'Open ye *the* gates,
'That a just nation keeping faithfulness, may enter;
'*Him that is* of firm purpose thou keepest *in* peace, peace,*
'Because he trusts in Thee.
'Trust ye in Yahveh evermore,
'For in Yah-Yahveh *is* a rock of ages.
'For He has cast down those who dwelt on high;
'A lofty city,—He lays it low,
'He laid it low, even to *the* ground,
'He levels it with *the* very dust.
'*The* foot tramples her—*the* feet of *the* afflicted,—
'*The* steps of *the* helpless!
'Straight *is the* path for *the* righteous;
'A road-way for *the* righteous thou levellest evenly.
'Yea, *in the* path of thy judgments we waited for thee,
    O Yahveh!

Chapter XXVI. 8—16.

'To thy name and to *the* remembrance of thee *was our* soul's desire.
' *With* my soul I longed for thee by night,
' Yea, *with* my spirit within me I sought thee earnestly ;
' For when thy judgments *are* upon *the* earth,
' *The* inhabitants of *the* world learn righteousness.
' Should a wicked man be favoured, he learns not righteousness ;
' In a land of uprightness will he act perversely,
' And will not behold *the* majesty of Yahveh !
' Uplifted was thy hand, Yahveh !—they saw it not !
' But they shall see *the* jealousy for *the* people and be ashamed,
' Yea, a fire shall devour thy foes.

' Yahveh ! Thou wilt ordain peace for us,
' For Thou too has wrought all our works for us.
' Yahveh, our Elohim ! Lords beside thee have ruled over us ;
' Only through thyself do we commemorate thy name ;
' Dead, they revive not—
' Shades, they do not arise !
' For this was it that thou didst visit and destroy them,
' And madest all their memory to perish.

' Yahveh ! thou hast increased *the* nation,
' Thou hast increased *the* nation and art glorified,
' Thou hast widened all *the* borders of *the* land.
' Yahveh ! in distress to thee they looked—

CHAPTERS XXVI. 15. XXVII. 1, 2.

'Thy chastening on them, they poured out whispered
    prayers;
'As when a pregnant woman draws nigh to *the* birth,
'Travails, cries out in her throes,
'So have we been in thy sight, Yahveh!
'We have been with child, have travailed,
'We brought forth as it were wind,
'We wrought not deliverance *for the* land,
'And inhabitants of *the* land were not born.
'Thy dead shall live—
'My dead bodies shall arise:
'Awake and sing ye dwellers in dust,
'For thy dew is a dew of herbs,
'And Earth shall give birth to *the* shades."
Go, my people, enter thy chambers,
And close thy door after thee;
Hide thee as for a little moment,
Till indignation be overpast.
For lo! from his place Yahveh comes forth,
To visit *the* sin of earth's inhabitants upon them,
And the earth shall disclose her bloodshed,
And shall cover her slain no longer.

In that day Yahveh visits with his sword,
The hard and the great and the powerful,
Leviathan, fleet serpent,
Leviathan, coiled serpent,
And slays the dragon which is in *the* sea.

In that day sing ye of 'the lovely vineyard,'

Chapter XXVII. 3—11.

'I, Yahveh, am its keeper—every moment do I water it—
'Lest any harm it, I keep it night and day.
'My anger is gone:
'Would that I had in battle thorns and briars—
'I would rush on them, would burn them together!
'Or *else* let any one lay hold on my protection,
'Let him make peace with me,
'Peace let him make with me.'
In the coming *days* Jacob shall strike root,
Israel shall bloom and bud,
And they fill *the* face of *the* world with fruit.

Hath He smitten him as He smote his smiter?*
Is he slain as his slayers were slain?
In measur*ed*-measure, in putting her away, didst thou contend with her,
He took her away with his rough blast in a day of east wind:
Therefore by this shall *the* guilt of Jacob be expiated,
And this, all *the* fruit of putting away his sin,
When he makes all altar-stones like pounded chalk-stones,
So that Asherahs and sun-pillars stand no longer.
For a *once* fortified city becomes solitary,
An abode unpeopled, and deserted like a wilderness:
There shall pasture, and there lie down *the* calf,
And it consumes its branches!
When its boughs are dry they are broken off,
Women come and kindle them.

THE PROPHECIES OF ISAIAH. 67

CHAPTER XXVII. 11—13.

For it is not a people of understanding,
Therefore their Maker pities them not,
And he that formed them shews them no favour.

And it comes to pass in that day,
That Yahveh will beat out corn,
From *the* flood * of Euphrates to *the* torrent of Egypt,
And ye, sons of Israel, shall be gleaned one by one ;
And it comes to pass in that day,
That a great trumpet shall be blown,
And they who were perishing in *the* land of Assyria come,
And the outcasts in *the* land of Egypt,
And they worship Yahveh,
On *the* holy mount in Jerusalem.

CHAPTERS XXVIII. XXXIII.

Denunciations delivered in the time of Sargon, B.C. 722, *against Ephraim and the ten tribes and Jerusalem. The alliance with Egypt. The Assyrian invaders. A prosperous reign (of Hezekiah), and a new era, xxxii. 1—8, with an address to women. Retribution upon Assyria (in the 26th year of Hezekiah,* B.C. 701.*)*

CHAPTER XXVIII. 1.

Woe to the proud crown of Ephraim's drunkards,
And *the* fading flower, his glorious beauty,
Which *is* on *the* head of *the* fat valley of *the* wine-smitten !

Chapter XXVIII. 2—9.

See! Adonai has a strong and a powerful one,
Like a storm of hail—a destroying tempest—
Like a storm of mighty waters, overwhelming,
With *force of* hand He casts down to *the* earth!
Under foot shall it be trampled,—
Proud crown of Ephraim's drunkards :—
And *the* fading flower, his glorious beauty
Which is on *the* head of *the* fat valley,
Shall be as an early fig before the fruit-season,
Which, whoso sees it, swallows as soon as it is in his hand.
In that day Yahveh Sabaoth shall be a crown of beauty,
And a diadem of glory to *the* residue of his people ;
And a spirit of judgment to him who sits on the judgment-seat,
And for strength to those who turn back *the* battle to *the foeman's* gate.

Yet even these stagger through wine,
And reel through strong drink :
Priest and prophet stagger through strong drink,
They are swallowed up by wine,
Through strong drink they reel,
They reel in vision, they totter in judgment :
For all tables are full of filthy vomit—
No place is left.

' Whom,' *say they*, ' would He teach knowledge ?
' And whom make to understand *the* message ?
' Those weaned from milk ?

CHAPTER XXVIII. 9—16.

'Those taken from *the* breasts?
'For *it is* "precept on precept, precept on precept,
' " Rule on rule, rule on rule,
' " A little here, a little there." '

But, with barbarous lip and a strange tongue,
Will He speak to this people :
For He said to them : 'This is the rest; rest ye *the* weary ;
'And this is the tranquillity,'—
Yet they would not hearken :
Therefore shall *the* word of Yahveh be to them,
'Precept on precept, precept on precept,
'Rule on rule, rule on rule,
'A little here, a little there,'
That they may go on, and stumble backward and be broken,
And be snared and taken.

Hear therefore, ye men of scorn, *the* word of Yahveh,
Rulers of this people which *is* in Jerusalem ;
Because ye said, 'We have struck a covenant with death,
'And have made a league with Sheol ;
'An overflowing scourge shall not reach us, as it passes along,
'For we have made a lie our refuge,
'And in falsehood have we hidden ourselves : "—
Therefore thus saith *the* Lord Yahveh,
Lo, I am He that hath founded a stone in Zion,

Chapter XXVIII. 16—25.

A proved stone, a costly corner-stone,
A founded foundation—
He who confides *in it* shall not flee hastily.
And I appoint right for a *measuring*-line,
And justice for a plummet,
And hail shall sweep away *the* refuge of a lie,
And waters shall overwhelm *the* hiding place,
And your covenant with death shall be cancelled,
And your league with Sheol shall not stand :
The overflowing scourge when it passes along—
—Then shall ye be to it for a trampling—
As oft as it passes along shall it take you away,
For it shall pass along every morning,
By day and by night ;
And it is even a terror to know *the* rumour *of it ;*
For the bed is too short to stretch in,
And too narrow the coverlet to wrap one's self in ;
For as *on* Mount Perazim will Yahveh uprise,
Will be wroth as *in the* valley of Gibeon,
To do his deed, his strange deed,
And work his work, his strange work.
Now then be ye not scoffers,
Lest your bonds be made strong ;
For I have heard of a final and decisive *doom,*
From Adonai Yahveh Sabaoth upon all the land.

Give ye ear and hear my voice,
Attend and hear my speech.
Does the plowman plough all day that he may sow ;
Open and harrow his ground ?

CHAPTERS XXVIII. 25—29.—XXIX. 1—4.

Does he not, when he has levelled its surface,
Cast abroad dill and scatter cummin,
And set wheat *in* rows,
And barley *in* its appointed place,
And vetch *in* its border?
For One instructs him aright,
His Elohim teaches him.
For not with sharp-sledge is dill threshed out,
Nor is a cart wheel rolled over cummin,
But dill is beaten out with staff,
And cummin with rod.
Bread-corn is trodden out;
Yet a man will not be always threshing it,
Nor urging *the* wheel of his wain and his horses—
He does not crush it.
This, too, proceeds from Yahveh Sabaoth,
He makes counsel wondrous, makes wisdom great.

Ah! God's Lion, God's Lion,
City where David camped!
Add year to year,
Let festivals go their round—
Then will I bring distress upon 'God's Lion,'
And there shall be moaning and bemoaning,*
Yet shall it be to me as a Lion-of-God.
For *though* I encamp against thee round about,
And lay siege to thee with a mound,
And set up forts against thee,
And, brought low, thou speakest from *the* ground,
And from *the* dust thy speech sighs forth,

Chapter XXIX. 4—10.

And thy voice comes out of *the* ground like a necromancer's,
And thy speech chirps from *the* dust,
Yet *the* multitude of thy foes shall become like small dust,
And *the* multitude of *the* terrible like flitting chaff,
And suddenly in a moment shall it take place.
By Yahveh Sabaoth will she be visited,
With thunder and with earthquake and a great shout,*
With storm and tempest and flame of devouring fire ;
And *the* multitude of all the nations that war against *the* Lion-of-God,
And all that go to war against her and her ramparts and who beleaguer her,
Shall be like a dream, a vision of night ;
And it shall be as when the hungry dreams, and see, he eats,—
But he wakes and his soul is empty :
And as when the thirsty dreams, and see, he drinks,—
But he wakes, and see, he is faint, and his soul is craving ;
So shall be *the* multitude of all the nations
Which go to war against Mount Zion.

Wait ye and be astonished ! *
Blind yourselves, and be blind !
They are drunken, but not with wine ;
They reel, but not with strong drink !
For Yahveh has poured out upon you a spirit of slumber,

Chapter XXIX. 10—16.

And has closed up your eyes, the prophets,
And your heads, the seers, has he covered over,
So that the whole vision has become to you
Like words of a sealed writing,
Which they deliver to one versed in writing, saying
  'Read now this,'
And he answers, 'I cannot, for it is sealed :'
And if the writing is delivered to one who is not versed
  in writing, saying, ' Read thou this,'
And he answers, 'I am not versed in writing ; '
Therefore saith Adonai,
Because this people draw near to me,
And with their mouth and lips honour me while their
  heart is far from me,
And their fear of me *is* a men-taught precept ;
Therefore, behold, I deal yet further with this people
  in marvellous sort,
Dealing marvellously and *with* marvel,
And *the* wisdom of their wise perishes,
And *the* skill of their skilful hides itself !
Woe to those who hide deep *their* purpose from Yahveh,
So that their works are in *the* dark,
And they say, ' Who sees us ? ' and ' Who notices us ? '
Perverse that ye are ! Shall the potter be regarded as
  clay,
So that a thing made shall say of its maker, ' He made
  me not ? '
And a thing fashioned say of its fashioner, ' He has no
  skill ? '

CHAPTERS XXIX. 18—24.—XXX. 1, 2.

Is it not yet a very little while,
Before Lebanon shall be changed into fruitful-land,
And the fruitful land be accounted a thicket?
And in that day the deaf hear *the* words of a writing,
And out of gloom and darkness *the* eyes of *the* blind see,
And *the* meek increase their joy in Yahveh,
And *the* poor among men exult in Israel's Holy One.
For a terrible one is no more,
A scoffer is destroyed,
And all watchers for iniquity are cut off,
Who condemn a man for a *single* word,
And lay snares for him that pleads in *the* gate,
And turn aside *the* just for nought.
Therefore thus saith Yahveh of *the* house of Jacob,
He Who delivered Abraham—
Now shall Jacob not be ashamed,
And his face shall not now grow pale;
For when he sees his children, *the* work of my hands, in his midst:
They shall hallow my name,
And hallow Jacob's Holy One,
And tremble at *the* Elohim of Israel,
And they who erred in spirit shall know prudence,
And murmurers shall learn instruction.

Ah! perverse sons!—it is an oracle of Yahveh,
To execute a purpose which is not of me,
To sanction a league by libation, but without my spirit,
That they may add sin to sin!
Who set forth to go down to Egypt,

CHAPTER XXX. 2—9.

But enquire not at my mouth;
To flee for refuge to *the* fortress of Pharaoh,
And to take refuge in Egypt's shadow!
Therefore will the fortress of Pharaoh become your disgrace,
And your refuge in Egypt's shadow, confusion.
For *when* his princes are at Zoan,
And his ambassadors arrive at Hanes,
Everyone will be ashamed of a people that cannot profit them,
Who are neither for help nor for profit,
But for shame and also for reproach.

The oracle concerning *the* beasts of *the* South.
Through a land of distress and difficulty,
Whence lioness and lion do come,
Viper and flying serpent :
They carry their wealth on shoulder of young asses,
And their treasures on hump of camels,
To a people that cannot profit.
Yea, the Egyptians—vapour and emptiness is their help—
Therefore I name it—' Arrogance, the inactive.'

Now go, write it on a tablet before them,
And record it on a scroll,
That it may be for a future day—
For a witness for ever.
For it is a rebellious people, lying sons,
Sons who refuse to hear *the* teaching of Yahveh,

Chapter XXX. 10—17.

Who say to seers, 'See not;'
And to beholders of visions, 'Behold not right things
    for us,
'Speak to us smooth things—Behold delusions—
'Withdraw from *the* way—Turn aside from *the* path—
'Cause the Holy One of Israel to cease from before us.
Wherefore thus saith *the* Holy One of Israel;
Because ye reject this word,
And trust in oppression and perverseness, and lean
    thereon,
Therefore shall this offence be to you
Like a falling breach, bulging in a lofty wall,
Whose breaking comes suddenly in a moment;
And he breaks it as one breaks a potter's vessel,
Dashing in pieces without sparing,
So that among its fragments not a sherd *is found*,
For taking fire from hearth, or for drawing water from
    cistern.
For thus said Adonai Yahveh, Israel's Holy One,
'In returning and quietness shall be your safety,
'In quietness and confidence shall be your strength;'
But ye would not, and said,
'No, for on horse will we flee;'
—Therefore shall ye flee—
'And on *the* swift will we ride!'
—Swift therefore shall be your pursuers.
One thousand at rebuke of one,
At rebuke of five shall ye flee,
Till ye be left like signal pole on the mountain top,
And like banner on the hill.

THE PROPHECIES OF ISAIAH.

CHAPTER XXX. 17—25.

And yet will Yahveh long to shew you favour,
And yet will He be on high to take pity on you,
For an Elohim of Justice is Yahveh,
Blessed all who long for Him !
For, O people who dwellest in Zion, in Jerusalem,
Thou shalt weep no more ;
At voice of your outcry He will shew you favour ;
When He hears it, He answers you.
And though Adonai give you distress as bread,
And oppression as water,
Yet shall thy teacher no more have to hide himself,
But your eyes constantly behold your teacher ;
And your ears hear a word from behind you, saying,
'This is the way, walk ye therein,'
When ye turn to the right, and when ye turn to the left.
Then ye defile the overlaying of your images of silver,
And the plating of your golden idols ;
Thou shalt scatter them as a loathsome thing,
Thou wilt say to it, ' Begone.'
Then gives He rain upon thy seed,
With which thou sowest the ground,
And bread, *the* produce of the ground—
It shall be nourishing and rich :
In that day thy cattle will feed in a broad pasture,
The oxen also, and the young asses that till the ground,
Will eat fermented provender
Which has been winnowed with fork and fan.
And on every high mountain and on every lofty hill
Are streams that run with water,—

Chapter XXX. 25—32.

In *the* day of a great slaughter, when towers fall.
And *the* light of the moon is as sun-light,
And the sun-light is sevenfold,
As light of seven days,
In *the* day when Yahveh binds up the breach of his people,
And heals *the* wound of their stroke.

Lo! *the* name of Yahveh comes from far!
His wrath burning,—
And mighty *the* towering flame;
His lips are full of indignation,
And his tongue like a devouring fire,
And his breath like an overflowing torrent,
Which divides at the neck,
To sift nations in a sieve of destruction,
And on *the* cheeks of nations is a misguiding bridle.
But ye shall have the song, as in a night when a Feast is celebrated,
And joy of heart, like one who walks to a pipe,
To come to Yahveh's Mount, to Israel's Rock.
Then Yahveh causes his glorious voice to be heard,
And a lighting down of his arm to be seen,
With fury of anger and flame of devouring fire,
With storm of flood and hailstone.
For at Yahveh's voice shall Asshur be broken down,
When with rod He smites him:
And every overpassing of destined scourge
Which Yahveh shall bring down upon him,
Is with tabrets and with harps—

CHAPTER XXX. 33.—XXXI. 1—4.

And with battles swaying to and fro, He fights against them.
For a place of burning has been prepared beforehand,
Even for *the* King is it made ready ;
He has deepened, has widened *it*,*
Its pile is fire and wood in abundance :
Breath of Yahveh, like a stream of sulphur, kindles it.

Ah ! the goers down to Egypt for help !
And on horses will they rely,
And trust in chariots, because they are many,
And in horsemen, because they are very strong,
But look not to *the* Holy One of Israel,
And enquire not of Yahveh !
Yet He, too, is wise,
And will bring on evil and withdraws not his words,
But arises against *the* house of evil doers,
And against helpers of those who work iniquity.
For Egyptians are men and not God,
And their horses flesh and not spirit :
And when Yahveh shall stretch out his hand
The helper stumbles and *the* holpen falls,
And all come to an end together.
For thus saith Yahveh to me.
As the lion and the young lion growls over his prey,
Against whom a band of shepherds is summoned,
—At their shout he is not dismayed,
Nor is he daunted at their crowd—
So Yahveh Sabaoth comes down to fight
Upon Mount Sion and upon her hill :—

CHAPTER XXXI. 5—9. XXXII. 1—4.

Like birds hovering *over their young*,
So will Yahveh Sabaoth defend Jerusalem,
Sheltering and delivering, passing over and rescuing.
Return to Him from whom ye have deeply revolted,
O Sons of Israel.

For in that day they will reject with scorn
Every man his vain-gods of silver and his vain-gods of gold,
Which your hands have made to you *for* a sin.
And Asshur falls by no human sword,
And a sword of no earth-born-man devours him ;
And he betakes him to flight from before *the* sword,
And his youths become tribute-payers,
And his rock will pass away through terror,
And his princes are dismayed at a signal :—
An oracle of Yahveh, who has his fire in Sion
And his furnace in Jerusalem.

Behold a king shall reign for justice,
And as for princes, they shall rule for right,
And each is as a hiding-place from wind,
And *like* a covert from rain-storm ;
Like streams of water in a parched ground,
Like *the* shadow of a great rock in a fainting land.
And *the* eyes of those that see shall not be dimmed,
And *the* ears of those who hear shall hearken,
And *the* heart of the hasty shall learn knowledge,
And *the* tongue of stammerers be prompt to speak clearly.

THE PROPHECIES OF ISAIAH. 81

CHAPTER XXXII. 5—14.

A fool shall no longer be called noble,
And a knave shall no longer be called gentle *in rank*,
For a fool will speak folly,
And his heart work wickedness,
Acting profanely and speaking error concerning Yahveh ;
Emptying *the* soul of *the* hungry
And he causes *the* drink of *the* thirsty to fail.
And as for a mean man, his means are evil :*
He devises mischiefs,
To ruin *the* humble with words of falsehood,
Even when *the* plea of *the* poor is just ;
But a generous man devises generous things,
And in generous things will he persist.

Rise up, ye women who are at ease ! hear my voice !
Ye confident daughters, give ear to my speech !
Let a year pass, and ye shall quake ye confident ones,
For vintage fails, ingathering comes not.
Tremble, ye that are at ease !
Quake, ye confident ones !
Strip, and make you bare,
And gird *sackcloth* on loins !

The men are smiting their bosom for *the* pleasant fields,*
For *the* fruitful vine !
On *the* land of my people thorns *and* briers come up,
Yea on all houses of joy *in the* exulting city.
For *the* palace will be deserted,
The tumult of the city be gone ;
Ophel and watchtower become as caverns for aye,

CHAPTER XXXII. 14—20. XXXIII. 1—3.

A joy of wild asses, a pasturage of flocks,
Till a spirit from on high be poured out upon us,
And a desert become a fruitful land,
And a fruitful land be counted for a forest ;
Then Right abides in *the* wilderness
And Justice inhabits *the* fruitful field ;
And the result of the justice is peace,
And the effect of the justice, quietness and assurance for ever ;
And my people will dwell in an abode of peace,
And in dwellings of confidence and in quiet resting places.
Yet *there is* a hail-fall at *the* falling of a forest,*
And in a low place will the city sink down low.
Blessed ye who sow by all waters,
Who set loose *the* foot of the ox and of the ass !

Woe to thee despoiler, and thou not despoiled !
And a plunderer, and thou not plundered !
When thou hast ceased from despoiling, thou shalt be despoiled,
When thou hast made an end of plundering, they shall plunder thee.

Yahveh ! be gracious to us : on Thee we wait :
Be Thou their arm every morning,—
Our safety also in time of distress.

At sound of tumult, *the* peoples flee :
When Thou upliftest Thyself, nations are scattered ;

CHAPTER XXXIII. 4—14.

And your spoil is gathered as the caterpillar-locust gathers,
As *winged* locusts run, they run upon it.

Exalted is Yahveh, for He dwells on high,
He fills Sion with judgment and justice ;
And *the* security of thy times is wealth of deliverances,
And of wisdom and knowledge ;
Fear of Yahveh, this his treasure.

See, *the* warriors raise a cry without—
Ambassadors of peace are weeping bitterly—
Highways lie desolate,
The wayfarer ceases—
He violates covenant, despises cities,
Regards not man :
The land wails, languishes,
Lebanon is shamed, withers,
The Sharon is become like a desert,
And Bashan and Carmel shake off *their leaves*.
Now will I arise, saith Yahveh,
Now will I exalt, now uplift myself ;
Ye conceive chaff, ye bring forth stubble,—
Your own breath a fire which devours you ;
So that nations become *as* burnings of lime,
Thorns cut up which are burned in fire !
Hear, *ye that are* far off, what I have wrought,
And *ye that are* near, acknowledge my might.

Sinners in Sion quake :
Trembling seizes on *the* impious ;

Chapter XXXIII. 14—24.

—" Who can sojourn with devouring fire ?
" Who can sojourn with perpetual burnings ? "
He who walks justly, and speaks aright,
Scorning lucre of oppression,
Shaking his hands from grasp of bribes,
Stopping his ears from hearing of bloodshed,
And shutting his eyes from beholding evil—
He dwells on high,
Strongholds of rocks his fortress,
His bread is given him, his waters are sure.
Thine eyes will behold a king in his splendour,
Will see *the* land to its full extent.

Thy heart will muse upon *the* alarm ;—
" Where is he who counted ? where he who weighed *the tribute ?*
" Where he who counted the towers ? "
The fierce people thou shalt see no more,
A people of speech too dark for hearing,
Of barbarous tongue, not to be understood.
Look upon Sion, city of our festivals ;
Thine eyes shall behold Jerusalem, a quiet dwelling,
A tent that will not remove,
Its tent-pegs never will be plucked up,
Nor any of its cords be broken.
But there Yahveh is in splendour for us—
A place of rivers, streams of ample breadth :
No oared galley shall pass upon it,
Nor splendid ship shall traverse it ;
For Yahveh our judge,

THE PROPHECIES OF ISAIAH.

Chapter XXXIII. 22—24.

Yahveh our lawgiver,
Yahveh our king—
He will deliver us.

Thy tacklings have been slackened ;
The foot of their mast they cannot strengthen ;—
They spread not out a signal ;
Yet even then is spoil shared in abundance,
Even the lame prey a prey,
And no inhabitant says, "I am sick : "
The people that dwell therein has its iniquity forgiven.

CHAPTERS XXXIV. XXXV.

Chapter XXXIV. 1—3.

The downfall of enemies, especially of Edom. The return of Israel, and their joy. Probably written early in the Captivity.

Draw nigh ye nations to hear,
And attend, ye peoples :
Let the earth and her fulness hear,
The world and all its offspring.
For Yahveh has indignation against all the nations,
And wrath against all their armies ;
He has laid a ban upon them, has given them up to slaughter,
And their slain are cast forth—

Chapter XXXIV. 3—11.

And *as for* their carcases—a stench from them goes up,—
And *the* mountains flow down with their blood,
And all *the* host of the Heavens melts away,
And the Heavens roll together like a scroll,
And all their host fades, as fades leaf from vine,
And like fading leaf from fig-tree.
For my sword has been made drunk in Heaven—
See! it descends on Edom,
And for judgment, on a people of my ban!
The sword of Yahveh is glutted with blood,
It is besmeared with fat,
With blood of lambs and he goats,
With fat of kidneys of rams:
For Yahveh has a sacrifice in Bozrah,
And a great slaughter in *the* land of Edom:
And with them will fall *the* buffaloes,
And bullocks with bulls;
And their land is drunken with blood,
And their soil is soaked with fat.
For Yahveh has a day of vengeance,
A year of requitals for Sion's quarrel.

And *Edom's* rivers are turned into pitch,
And her dust into brimstone;
And her land becomes burning pitch,
—Night and day it is unquenched—
Her smoke ascends for ever,
From generation to generation it lies waste,
None pass through it for ever and ever.
And pelican and hedgehog possess it,

CHAPTERS XXXIV. 11—17. XXXV. 1.

And owl and raven dwell therein,
And one stretches over it a line of ruin,
And a plummet of emptiness.
As for her nobles—none is there whom they can call *to* the rule,
And all her princes come to nought,
And thorns spring up *in* her palaces,
Nettle and thistle in her fortresses,
And she is become a dwelling-place of jackals,
An enclosure for daughters of *the* ostrich,
And jackals meet wolves,
And Satyr will call to his fellow :
There too rests Lilith,
And finds for herself a place of repose :
There nestles arrow-snake and lays,
And hatches, and gathers under her shadow :
There too are kites assembled,
Each *with* her mate :
Search out from Yahveh's scroll and read—
Not one of these is missing,
None lacks its mate.
For *Yahveh's* mouth—it has commanded,
And His breath—it has mustered them ;
And He has cast a lot for them,
And His hand has measured it out to them by line,
They will occupy it for ever,
From generation to generation will they dwell therein.

At this a wilderness and a dry land rejoices,
And a desert exults and blossoms like *the* narcissus,

Chapter XXXV. 2—10.

It blossoms and exults even *with* joy and shouting.
The Lebanon's glory is given to it,
The Carmel's and the Sharon's splendour;
They will see *the* glory of Yahveh, *the* splendour of our Elohim.
Strengthen ye *the* feeble hands,
And tottering knees make firm;
Say to *the* timid of heart, 'Be strong, fear ye not;
'Behold your Elohim—vengeance will come— retribution of Elohim—
'He will come and deliver you.'
Then opened will be *the* blind men's eyes,
And ears of *the* deaf unstopped;
Then will *the* lame man bound like a hart,
And *the* tongue of *the* dumb shout aloud;
For waters have broken out in a wilderness,
And rivers in a desert;
And the mirage becomes a lake,
And a thirsty land springs of water:
In *the* haunt of jackals, *where* they crouch,
Is a bed for reed and bulrush.
And a high-road and a way is there,
And it will be called 'the holy way;'
The unclean pass not over it, since it is for them—*His people*,
And wayfarers, though fools, will not go astray,
No lion will be there, nor ravenous beasts mount it,
It will not be found there,
But *there* journey the redeemed,
And Yahveh's ransomed ones will return,

CHAPTERS XXXV. 10.   XXXVI. 1—7.

And they come to Zion with shouting
And perpetual joy on their heads :
They will obtain gladness and joy,
And sorrow and sighing flee away.

▼▼▼▼▼▼▼▼▼▼▼▼▼▼▼▼▼▼▼▼▼▼▼▼▼

CHAPTERS XXXVI. XXXIX.

Compare 2 Kings xviii. 13—xx. 19.

CHAPTER XXXVI. 1—7.

And it came to pass in *the* fourteenth year of king Hezekiah, Sennacherib king of Assyria came up against all the fortified towns of Judah and took them. And the king of Assyria sent Rabshakeh from Lachish to Jerusalem, with a great force, to the king Hezekiah ; and he halted at *the* conduit of the upper pool, on *the* highway of *the* fuller's field. Then there went out to him Eliakim, son of Hilkiah, the house steward, and Shebna the scribe, and Joah, son of Asaph, the recorder.

And Rabshakeh said to them : Say now to Hezekiah, thus says the great king, the king of Assyria, What confidence is this in which you confide ? I say that your counsel and might for war is a mere thing of *the* lips. On whom now do you rely that you rebel against me ? Behold ! you confide in this staff of a broken reed, on Egypt ; which, if a man lean on it, will go into his hand and pierce it : such is Pharoah king of Egypt to all who confide on him. But if you say to me, We rely on Yahveh our Elohim : is it not He, whose high places and whose

Chapter XXXVI. 7—16.

altars Hezekiah has taken away, and said to Judah and Jerusalem, Before this altar shall ye worship? But now, engage with my master the king of Assyria: and I will give you two thousand horses, if you are able to furnish for yourself riders on them. How then will you turn away the face of one commander of the least of my master's servants? And yet you rely for yourself on Egypt for chariots and horsemen! But now, is it without Yahveh that I have come up against this land to destroy it? Yahveh said to me, Go up against this land, and destroy it.

Then said Eliakim and Shebna and Joah to Rabshakeh, Speak, we pray you, to your servants in Aramean, for we understand it, but speak to us not in Jewish, in *the* hearing of the people who are on the wall. But Rabshakeh said: Has my master sent me to your master and to you, to speak these words, and not to the men who are sitting on the wall, that they may eat their own filth, and drink their own urine with you?

And Rabshakeh stood up, and called out in a loud voice in Jewish, and said: Hear the words of the great king, king of Assyria. Thus says the king: Let not Hezekiah deceive you, for he is not able to deliver you; and let not Hezekiah cause you to confide in Yahveh, saying, Yahveh will certainly deliver us; this city will not be given into the hand of *the* king of Assyria. Listen not to Hezekiah: for thus says the king of Assyria: Make a treaty with me, and come out to me; and eat ye, each of his vine and each of his fig-tree; and drink ye each,

CHAPTERS XXXVI. 16—22. XXXVII. 1—4.

waters of his cistern, until I come and take you to a land like your own land, a land of corn and of new wine, a land of bread and of vineyards. Let not Hezekiah urge you, saying, Yahveh will deliver us. Have *the* Elohim of the nations delivered each his own land from *the* hand of *the* king of Assyria? Where are *the* Elohim of Hamath and of Arpad? Where are *the* Elohim of Sepharvaim? And did *its gods* deliver Samaria from my hand? Who among all *the* Elohim of these lands has delivered their land from my hand, that Yahveh should deliver Jerusalem from my hand? But they kept silent, and answered him not a word : for the king's order was, Answer him not.

Then Eliakim, son of Hilkiah, the house steward, and Shebna, the scribe, and Joah, the son of Asaph the recorder, came to Hezekiah with rent clothes, and told him the words of Rabshakeh. And it came to pass, when king Hezekiah heard it, he rent his clothes and covered himself with sackcloth, and went to *the* house of Yahveh. And he sent Eliakim, the house steward, and Shebna the scribe, and elders of the priests, covered with sackcloth, to Isaiah son of Amoz the prophet. And they said to him, Thus says Hezekiah : A day of distress and reproof and insult is this day ; for children are come to birth, and there is not strength to bring forth. Yahveh thy Elohim will perhaps hear the words of Rabshakeh whom his master *the* king of Assyria has sent to blaspheme the living Elohim, and will smite for *the* words which Yahveh thy Elohim has heard : Wherefore lift up a prayer for the remnant which remains." And *the*

Chapter XXXVII. 5—16.

servants of king Hezekiah came to Isaiah ; and Isaiah said to them, 'Say thus to your master, Thus says Yahveh : Fear not on account of the words which you have heard, with which *the* servants of *the* king of Assyria have blasphemed me. Behold, I suggest a purpose to him, and he hears a rumour, and returns to his own land, and in his own land I cause him to fall by *the* sword.' And Rabshakeh went back, and found the king of Assyria besieging Libnah, for he had heard that he had broken up Lachish. And he heard of Tirhakah, king of Æthiopia, 'He is come forth to fight against you :' and when he heard it he sent messengers to Hezekiah, saying : Thus say to Hezekiah king of Judah, Let not your Elohim in whom you confide deceive you, saying, Jerusalem shall not be given into *the* hand of *the* king of Assyria. Behold you have heard what *the* kings of Assyria have done to all the lands, so as utterly to destroy them ; and shall you be delivered ? Have the Elohim of the nations delivered those whom my father destroyed ? Gozan, and Haran, and Rezeph, and the children of Eden which were in Telassar ? Where is the king of Hamath, and the king of Arphad, and the king of *the* city of Sepharvaim, of Henah and of Ivah ?"

And Hezekiah took the letter from *the* hand of the messengers, and read it ; and he went up to the house of Yahveh ; and Hezekiah spread it out before Yahveh : and Hezekiah prayed to Yahveh, saying, 'Yahveh of Hosts, Elohim of Israel, enthroned on cherubim, Thou art the very God, even Thou alone, of all *the* kingdoms of the

THE PROPHECIES OF ISAIAH. 93

Chapter XXXVII, 16—24.

earth; Thou hast made the Heavens and the Earth! Yahveh, bow down thine ear and hear; open, Yahveh, Thine eye and see; and hear all *the* words of Sennacherib, which he hath sent to reproach the living Elohim. In truth, Yahveh, *the* kings of Assyria have destroyed all the nations, and their lands, and their Elohim have they consigned to *the* fire, for no Elohim were they, but work of *the* hands of man, wood and stone, and destroyed them. And now, Yahveh our Elohim, save us from his hand, that all *the* kingdoms of the earth may know that Thou art Yahveh, Thou alone.'

Then Isaiah, son of Amoz, sent to Hezekiah, saying: Yahveh, the Elohim of Israel, says thus: 'That which thou hast prayed to me concerning Sennacherib king of Assyria, I have heard: This is the Word which Yahveh speaks against him:

The virgin-daughter of Zion scorns thee, laughs at thee;
Jerusalem's daughter shakes *her* head after thee.
Whom hast thou reproached and reviled,
And against whom hast thou uplifted voice,
And raised thine eyes on high?
—Against *the* Holy One of Israel.
By thy servants hast thou reproached Adonai and said;
' With a multitude of my chariots I have gone up
' To *the* mountain height, recesses of Lebanon,
' And have cut down its tallest cedars, its choicest
   cypresses,
' And I come into its utmost height, its garden-like
   forest :

Chapter XXXVII. 25—31.

'I have digged and drunk *its* waters,
'And with sole of my foot I dry up all *the* canals of Egypt.'

Hast thou not heard that I ordained it long ago,
In ancient days, and planned it?
I have now brought it about
That thou shouldest be to lay waste fortified cities *into* ruined heaps;
And their inhabitants *became* short of power,
Were broken down and confounded;
They became *like* grass of a field and green herbage,
Like blades on roofs,
And *plants* blasted ere grown.
But thy downsitting and thy outgoing and thy incoming I know,
And thy rage against me:
Because thy rage against me
And thy insolence is come up into my ears,
In thy nose will I put my hook, and in thy lips my bridle,
And will turn thee back in *the* way by which thou camest.

And to thee *O Prophet* is this the sign:—
One eateth this year the aftergrowth,
And in the second year what is self-sown,
And in a third year sow ye and reap,
And plant vineyards and eat their fruit.
And *the* escaped of *the* house of Judah who are left,
Root downward, and make fruit upward;

CHAPTER XXXVII. 32—38.

For from Jerusalem shall go forth a remnant,
And from Mount Zion *the* escaped :
The zeal of Yahveh Sabaoth will effect this.
Therefore thus saith Yahveh of Assyria's king,
Into this city he shall not come,
Nor shoot arrow there,
Nor present shield before it,
Nor cast up mound against it,
By *the* way that he comes, by it shall he return,
And into this city he shall not come,
—It is the utterance of Yahveh—
And I protect this city to deliver it,
For my own sake and David my servant's sake.'

And an angel of Yahveh went forth and smote in *the* camp of Assyria 185,000 ; and when *men* arose early in *the* morning, behold they were all dead corpses. Then Sennacherib king of Assyria broke up and departed and returned, and abode in Nineveh : and it came to pass, as he was worshipping *in the* house of Nisroch his Elohim, Adrammelech and Sharezer his sons smote him with *the* sword : and they escaped into *the* land of Ararat : and Esarhaddon his son reigned in his stead.

━━━━━━━━━━━━━━━━━━━━━.

CHAPTER XXXVIII. 1.

In those days Hezekiah was sick unto death. And Isaiah the prophet, son of Amoz, came to him and said to him ; Thus saith Yahveh : Give charge to

CHAPTER XXXVIII. 2—10.

thy household, for thou shalt die and not live.' Then Hezekiah turned his face to the wall, and prayed to Yahveh ; and he said, ' Ah, Yahveh, remember now, I
' beseech thee, how I have walked before thee in truth
' and with a devoted heart, and have done what was
' good in thine eyes ;' and Hezekiah wept a great weeping. Then a word from Yahveh came to Isaiah, saying, ' Go and say to Hezekiah, Thus saith Yahveh,
' *the* Elohim of David thy father : I have heard thy
' prayer ; I have seen thy tears : Behold, I add to thy
' days fifteen years: And out of *the* palm of *the* king
' of Assyria will I deliver thee and this city, and I will
' protect this city. And Isaiah said : Let them bring a
' cake of figs, and let them bind to the boil, that he may
' live. And Hezekiah said : What is the sign that I
' shall go up to *the* house of Yahveh ? And this the
' sign to thee from Yahveh, that Yahveh will effect this
' word which he has spoken : Behold, I will turn
' the shadow of the degree-steps over which it has gone
' down by the sun on *the* degree-steps of Ahaz, ten
' degrees backward.' And the sun turned ten degrees backward, on *the* degree-steps *over* which it had gone down.

A writing of Hezekiah, King of Judah, when he had been sick, and was recovered from his sickness :

   I said : ' In *the* noon-tide stillness of my days
' I must go within *the* gates of Sheol,
' I am amerced of *the* remnant of my years."

CHAPTER XXXVIII. 11—17.

I said : 'No more shall I see Jah,
'Jah in *the* land of the living;
'Man shall I behold no more,
'*When* with them that have ceased to be :
'My life-time is plucked up and carried off from me like a shepherd's tent,
'I roll up my life like a weaver,
'From the warp he will cut me off—
'Within a day and night wilt thou bring me to an end.
'I cry for help till morn—
'As a lion, so will He break all my bones :
'Within a day and night wilt thou bring me to an end.
'Like a circling swallow, so will I shrill;
'Like a dove will I moan—
'My eyes languish *with looking* upwards :—
'O Yahveh! I am hard-pressed : undertake for me.'

What shall I say ?
He both promised me and Himself has performed it!
All my years shall I walk at ease,
After *the past* bitterness of my soul.
Adonai ! By these *things men* can live,
And there is in them for all, *that which is* the life of my spirit
For Thou hast restored me, and made me live.
Lo ! for *my* welfare *it was* bitter to me, bitter!
But Thou hast lovingly drawn my soul from *the* pit of destruction,
For Thou hast cast all my sins behind Thy back.

CHAPTER XXXVIII. 18—XXXIX. 4.

For Sheol cannot praise thee—
Death *cannot* celebrate thee,
They that go down into *the* pit cannot hope for thy faithfulness :
The living, *the* living, he can praise Thee,
As I *do* this day :—
Father to child can make known thy faithfulness !
Yahveh rescued me :—
Therefore will we strike our harps,
All *the* days of our life in Yahveh's house.

CHAPTER XXXIX. 1—4.

At that time Merodach Baladan, son of Baladan, king of Babylon, sent a letter and a present to Hezekiah, for he had heard that he had been sick and was recovered. And Hezekiah was glad because of them, and shewed them his treasure house, the silver and the gold, and the spices and the precious ointment, and all *the* house of his armour and all that was found in his treasures : there was not any thing in his house and in all his dominion which Hezekiah did not shew them. Then came Isaiah the prophet to the king Hezekiah and said to him : ' What said these men ? and whence come they to thee ? '

And Hezekiah said : ' They have come to me from a ' far country—from Babylon.' Then said he : ' What saw they in thy house ? ' And Hezekiah said, ' They ' have seen everything in my house ; there is nothing

Chapter XXXIX. 4—XL. 2.

'among my treasures which I have not shewn them.'
Then said Isaiah to Hezekiah, ' Hear *the* word of Yah-
' veh of Hosts: Behold, *the* days are coming when
' all that is thine house, and all that thy fathers have
' treasured up to this day, shall be carried off to Babylon:
' not a thing, saith Yahveh, shall be left. And of thy sons
' which shall issue from thee, whom thou shalt beget, shall
' they take, that they may become eunuchs in *the* palace
' of *the* king of Babylon.' And Hezekiah said to Isaiah:
' Good is *the* word of Yahveh which thou hast spoken.'
He said also: ' There will be peace and security in my
' days.'

CHAPTERS XL.--XLVI.

Revelations of the Return from Captivity, which all flesh in the great world-empires, especially Assyria and Babylon, shall witness. Contrasts between Yahveh and his people, and the false gods and their people: Cyrus the servant and anointed of Yahveh. Encouragements addressed to Israel, and to Cyrus. Idolatry rebuked.

'Comfort ye, comfort my people,'
Saith your Elohim.
'Speak ye to *the* heart of Jerusalem and proclaim to her,
That her warfare is fulfilled,
' That her iniquity is expiated,
' That she has received at Yahveh's hand double for all
her misdeeds.'

THE PROPHECIES OF ISAIAH.

Chapter XL. 3—11.

A voice proclaims—
' Prepare ye in *the* wilderness Yahveh's way,
' Level in *the* desert a highway for our Elohim!
' Let every valley be uplifted,
' And every mountain and hill be made low ;
' And let the steep become a level,
' And the rough places a plain ;
' And *the* glory of Yahveh shall be revealed,
' And all flesh behold together
' That Yahveh's mouth has spoken.'

A voice saith ' Proclaim : '
And *the prophet* said, ' What shall I proclaim ? '
' All the flesh is grass,
' And all its grace as a flower of the field :
' Withered *the* grass, faded *the* flower,
' For *the* breath of Yahveh has blown upon it ;
' Surely the people is grass !
' Withered *the* grass, faded *the* flower,
' But *the* word of our Elohim shall stand for ever.'
Zion, heraldess of joy, get thee up into a high mountain ;
Jerusalem, heraldess of joy, uplift thy voice with strength ;
Uplift *it*, be not afraid ;
Say to *the* cities of Judah, ' Behold your Elohim !
' Lo ! Adonai Yahveh will come like a valiant one,
' And his arm ruling for Him :
' Lo ! His reward with Him,
' And His recompence before Him !
' Like a shepherd will He shepherd His flock,

CHAPTER XL. 11—20.

' *The* lambs will He gather in His arm,
'And in His bosom carry *them*,
' *And* those that give suck will He lead.'

Who measured *the* waters in His palm,
And meted *the* heavens with a span,
And held *the* dust of the earth in a measure,
And weighed mountains in scales
And hills in a blance ?
Who has measured out the spirit of Yahveh,
And, *as* man of his counsel, taught Him ?
With whom took He counsel that he might instruct Him
And teach Him as to a path of right,
And teach Him knowledge,
And inform Him of a way of understanding ?
Lo ! nations as a drop from a bucket,
And as dust on a balance are reckoned :
Lo ! He lifts up countries as fine dust,
And Lebanon suffices not for fuel,
And its beasts suffice not for burnt offering ;
All the nations are before Him, as though *they were* not,
Are accounted by Him as nought and nothingness.
To what then can ye liken God [EL] ?
And what likeness will ye place beside Him ?

As to the image, a workman moulds *it*,
And a goldsmith overlays it with gold,
And casts for it chains of silver :—
Even a poor offerer chooses wood that will not rot,
He seeks him a skillful workman,

Chapters XL. 20—28.

To set up an image which shall not stir.
Can ye not perceive? can ye not hearken?
From *the* beginning has it not been told you?
Have ye not understood *from* earth's foundations?
He who sits above *the* vault of the earth,
And its inhabitants *are* as locusts;
Who stretches out *the* Heavens as fine cloth,
And spreads them out as a tent for dwelling;
He who turns princes to nothing,
He makes *the* judges of the earth nothingness:
Scarcely are they planted, scarcely are they sown,
Scarcely has their stem rooted in earth,
When He blasts them and they wither,
And a whirlwind bears them away as a stubble!
To whom then will ye liken Me, that I should resemble
    him? saith *the* Holy *One*.
Lift up your eyes on high and behold:
Who created these?
He who brings forth their host in number,
—He calls them all by name—
Through *His* great might, and being firm in prowess,
Not one is missing!

Why sayest thou, O Jacob, and speakest, O Israel,
My way is hidden from Yahveh,
And my cause is passed over by my Elohim?
Hast thou not known? hast thou not heard?
Yahveh is an everlasting Elohim?
Creator of *the* ends of the earth;
He faints not, neither is He weary;

CHAPTER XL. 28—XLI. 6.

Unsearchable is His understanding;
Giving vigour to *the* faint,
And to *the* powerless He increases strength:
And though youths may faint and be weary
And youthful warriors stumble;
Yet they who wait on Yahveh will renew *their* vigour
Uplift pinion like eagles,
Run and not weary,
Go on and not faint.

Keep silence towards me, O countries,
And let *the* nations take fresh strength:
Let them approach; then let them speak;
Let us draw near for judgment together.

Who has stirred up from *the* sun-rise
Him whose steps *God's* righteous dealing attends—
Gives up nations before him and subdues kings—
Makes their sword as dust,
Their bow as driven chaff?
He pursues them, passes on safely—
By a way his feet had never trodden:—
Who has wrought and done *this*?
He that called the generations from *the* beginning;
I, Yahveh, *the* first; and, with *the* last, *am* I the same.

The countries saw it, and are afraid *
The ends of the earth tremble;
They draw near and are come.
Each helps his fellow,

Chapter XLI. 6—14.

And saith to his brother, 'Be strong!'
And *the* graver encourages the smith,
He that smoothes with hammer, him that strikes on anvil,
Saying of *the* soldering, 'It *is* good:'
So he fastens it with nails that it stir not!

But thou, Israel, My servant,
Jacob whom I have chosen,
Seed of Abraham, My friend;
Thou whom I have supported from *the* ends of the earth,
And called from its borders,
And said to thee 'My servant, thou,
'I have chosen thee and not rejected thee;'
Fear not for I am with thee,
Look not around *for help*, for I am thy Elohim;
I strengthen thee, I also help thee,
I also uphold thee with my right hand of deliverance.
Lo! all that were enraged at thee, shall be ashamed and confounded;
Men that contended with thee, shall be as nought and perish:
Thou shalt seek them and not find them,—the men that strove with thee—
They shall become as nothing and as nought—*the* men that warred with thee.
For I, Yahveh thy Elohim, hold fast thy right hand,
I, who say to thee, Fear not; I help thee.
Fear not, worm Jacob, feeble folk of Israel,

CHAPTER XLI. 14—21.
—*It is the* utterance of Yahveh,— I help thee,
And thy Vindicator is *the* Holy One of Israel.
See ! I make thee a threshing sledge,
Sharp, new, furnished with teeth ;
Thou shalt thresh mountains and crush them,
And hills shalt thou make as chaff,
—Winnow them—and a blast carry them away,
And a tempest scatter them ;
But thou shalt rejoice in Yahveh,
And in Israel's Holy One shalt glory.

The afflicted and the needy are seeking water and there is none,
Their tongue is parched with thirst !
I, Yahveh, will answer them,
I, Elohim of Israel, will not forsake them ;
On bare hills will I open rivers,
And fountains in *the* midst of valleys ;
I will make a wilderness a pool of waters,
And a dry ground springs of water,
In *the* wilderness will I plant cedar, acacia,
And myrtle and wild olive ;
I will plant *the* cypress in *the* desert,
Pine and sherbin together,
That men may see and know,
And consider and understand at once,
That Yahveh's hand has done this,
And *the* Holy One of Israel has wrought it.

Bring near your cause, saith Yahveh ;

Chapter XLI. 21—28.

Produce your strong-proofs, saith *the* king of Jacob :
Let them produce *them* and announce to us what shall happen ;
Let them announce the former things, what they *be*,
That we may lay them to heart and mark their issue :
Or, cause us to hear of the things to come,
Tell what will come hereafter,
That we may know that ye are Elohim :
Yea, do good and do evil,
That we may gaze around and behold *it* together.
Lo, ye are of nothing,
And your work is of nought :
An abomination he that chooses you!

I have stirred up *one* from *the* north, and he is come—
From *the* rising of *the* sun, he proclaims My name :
And tramples on princes as on mortar,
And as a potter treads on clay ;
Who announced *this* from *the* beginning that we might know *it* ?
And, from aforetime, that we might say ' Right ? '
Yea, no one announced it,
Yea, no one caused it to be heard,
Yea, no one heard your words ;
I first *proclaimed* to Zion—Behold, Behold them—
And I give to Jerusalem a messenger of joy !

For I look, but there is no one ;
And out of these was no counsellor,
That I might ask them, and they give an answer.

THE PROPHECIES OF ISAIAH.

CHAPTER XLI. 29—XLII. 8.

Lo! they are all vanity,
Their works, nothingness,
Their images, wind and emptiness.

Behold! My servant whom I uphold,
My chosen, *in whom* My soul is well pleased!
I have put My spirit upon him,
He will cause law to go forth to *the* nations;
He will not clamour nor uplift *a cry*,
Nor cause His voice to be heard in the street;
He will not break a bruised reed,
Nor quench a faintly-burning wick,
He will bring forth a law in truth.
He shall not burn-dimly nor be broken down,
Till He have established a law in *the* earth,
And countries await His teaching.

Thus saith the El, Yahveh,
He who created the heavens and stretched them forth
Who spread out the earth and its produce,
Giving breath to *the* people upon it,
And spirit to those who walk therein:
I, Yahveh, have called thee in righteous dealing,
And will hold thy hand and keep thee,
And appoint thee for a covenant of *the* people,
For a light of nations;
To open blind eyes,
To bring forth captives from a dungeon,
And those who sit in darkness from a prison house.
I *am* Yahveh—this *is* My name—

Chapter XLII. 8—16.

And Hy glory I will not give to another,
Nor My praise to idols.
The former events, behold! are come to pass,
And new things do I announce,
Ere yet they spring up, I cause you to hear of them.

Sing ye to Yahveh a new song,
His praise from *the* ends of the earth,
Ye that go down to the sea, and its fulness;
Countries and their inhabitants.
Let *the* desert and its cities uplift *the* strain,
Villages where Kedar dwells:
Let *the* inhabitants of Sela shout,
Let them cry aloud from top of mountains,
Let them ascribe glory to Yahveh,
And declare his praise among *the* countries.
Yahveh goes forth like a champion,
Stirs up his jealousy like a man of wars,
Sounds an alarm, yea, raises a war-cry,
Shews himself mighty over His foes.

Long have I been silent, been still, and refrained Me,
But now I groan like a travailing woman,
Gasp and pant at once!
I lay waste mountains and hills,
And dry up all their herbage,
And I will turn rivers into mainlands,
And pools I dry up;
And I lead *the* blind by a way they knew not,
By paths they knew not I guide them,

CHAPTERS XLII. 16—24.

I make darkness into light before them,
And rough places into a level plain—
These the things I have done and have not left them
    undone.
They are driven back—they are utterly ashamed
Who trust in graven-images,
Who say to molten-images, ' Ye are our Elohim.'
Hear ye, deaf!
And look ye blind, that *ye may* see !
Who, but My servant, is blind ?
And deaf, as My messenger whom I send ?
Who is *so* blind as *the* devoted one,
And blind, as Yahveh's servant ?
Many things hast thou seen, but thou heedest not!
Having ears open, but he hears not !
Fain would Yahveh for His righteous-dealing sake
Make *His* teaching great and glorious ;
Yet this is a people spoiled and plundered,
They are all snared in holes,
And hidden in prison houses !
They have become a prey and there is no deliverer,
A plunder, and no one saith ' Restore ! '

Who among you will give ear to this,
Attend and hear for after-time ?
Who gave up Jacob for a prey
And Israel to plunderers ?
Did not Yahveh ? He against whom we had sinned,
And in whose ways they would not walk,
Nor hearken to His teaching ?

Chapter XLII. 25—XLIII. 6.

So he poured out upon him *the* hotness of his ire,
And violence of war;
And it kindled a flame around him, and he would not heed it,
And it set him on fire, and he would not lay it to heart.

But now, thus saith Yahveh, thy creator, O Jacob,
And He that formed thee, O Israel,
Fear not for I redeem thee,
I have called thee by thy name—thou *art* Mine—
When thou passest through waters I *am* with thee,
And through rivers, they shall not overflow thee;
When thou walkest through fire thou shalt not be scorched,
Nor shall flame set thee on fire.
For I, Yahveh, am thine Elohim,
Israel's Holy One, thy deliverer;
I give Egypt for thy ransom,
Cush and Seba in thy stead.
Since thou art precious in Mine eyes,
Honoured, and I love thee,
Therefore I give men in thy stead,
And peoples for thy life.
Fear not, for I am with thee,
From *the* sun-rise I bring thy seed
And gather you from *the* sunset:
To *the* north I say 'Give up,'
And to *the* south, 'Withhold not:'
Bring My sons from far,
And My daughters from *the* ends of the earth.

CHAPTER XLIII. 7—14.

Every one who is called by My name,
And whom I have created for My glory,
Whom I have formed, yea have made.

Bring forth a blind people who yet have eyes,
And deaf, who yet have ears!
Let all the nations be gathered together,
And let peoples be assembled :
Who among them could announce this!
And let them cause us to hear former things,
Let them produce their witnesses that they may be proved right,
That they may hearken, and say, ' Truth.'
Ye are My witnesses—*it is the* utterance of Yahveh—
And My Servant whom I have chosen,
That ye may acknowledge and believe Me,
And understand that I am He ;
Before Me was no God [EL] formed,
Neither shall be after Me.
I, I am Yahveh,
And beside Me *there is* no deliverer ;
I have announced and delivered and made it known,
And no strange *God* among you :
And ye are My witnesses—*it is the* utterance of Yahveh, and I am El : [the Strong One]
Yea from *this* day forth I am He,
And none can rescue from My hand :
I work, and who can reverse it ?
Thus saith Yahveh, your Vindicator,

CHAPTERS XLIII. 14—23.

The Holy One of Israel;
For your sakes have I sent to Babylon,
And I have brought down *the* barriers, all of them,
And Chaldees with the ships of their shouting,
I Yahveh, your Holy One,
Creator of Israel, your king.
Thus said Yahveh, He who makes a way in *the* sea
A path in mighty waters,
Who brings forth chariot and horse,
Army and might :—
They lie down together—they cannot arise—
Are extinguished—are quenched as a wick!
Remember not former things,
Nor consider things of old :
See I effect a new *thing*,
Even now it springs up : will ye not regard it?
Yea in a wilderness I make a road,
In a desert, streams :
Wild beasts of the field shall honour Me,
Jackals and ostriches
Because in a wilderness I give waters
And streams in a desert,
To give drink to My people, my chosen.
The people whom I have formed for Myself,
They shall recount My praise.

But upon Me thou hast not called, O Jacob!
Yea, O Israel, of Me thou hast been weary!
No sheep of thy burnt offerings hast thou brought Me,

CHAPTERS XLIII. 24—XLIV. 5.

Yet thou has bought Me with silver* no *scented* reed
Nor sated Me with fat of thy sacrifices,
But thou hast made Me toil with thy sins
And wearied Me with thine iniquities.

I, I am He who for My own sake blot out thy rebellions,
And will not remember thy sins.
Remind me : let us plead together :
Speak on, that thou mayest be cleared.
Thy chief father *Jacob* sinned,
And they who interceded for thee have rebelled against
   Me :—
I therefore profaned *the* princes of the sanctuary
And gave up Jacob to a ban,
And Israel to reproaches.

Yet now hearken, Jacob My servant,
And Israel, whom I have chosen :
Thus saith Yahveh who created thee,
And fashioned thee from *the* womb, *and* will help thee :
Fear not, My servant Jacob,
And thou, O upright-folk, whom I have chosen :
For I will pour waters on *the* thirsty,
And floods upon a dry ground ;
I will pour My spirit on thy seed,
And My blessing on thy offspring :
Then spring they up as amid grass,
As willows by brooks of water ;
This one shall say, ' I am Yahveh's,'
And this one shall call himself by *the name of* Jacob,

CHAPTER XLIV. 5—12.

And this one shall inscribe on his hand, 'For Yahveh,'
And surname himself by *the* name of Israel.

Thus saith Yahveh, Israel's king,
And Yahveh Sabaoth his vindicator:
I am First, and I Last,
And beside Me *there is* no Elohim!
For who can announce like Me,
—Let him declare it and set it out to Me—
Since I founded *the* people of old?
And future things and coming events let them announce.
Fear ye not, neither be afraid:
Have I not long since caused thee to hear, and declared
 it?
Ye are therefore my witnesses—
Is there an Eloah beside Me?
And there is no rock, I know not *any.*
Fashioners of idols are vanity, all of them,
The images in which they delight cannot profit,
And their witnesses have no vision,
Nor understand, that they may be ashamed.

Who has formed a god, or molten a profitless image?
See, all his associates are ashamed;
And *the* artificers who are but men,
Assemble themselves, take their stand,
Tremble, are ashamed at once!

A smith *sharpens* an axe,
And works it in charcoal and fashions it with hammers,

CHAPTER XLIV. 12—18.

And labours it with his strong arm :
He is hungry too, and has no strength,
He drinks no water, and is faint.
A carpenter stretches out a line,
He sketches it with a graver,
He works it with carving tools,
And with compass he marks it out,
And makes it like *the* figure of a man,
Like *the* beauty of a human-being,
To dwell in a shrine.
He sets him to hew down cedars for himself,
And takes holm-oak and oak,
And grows them for himself among forest trees ;
He plants a pine, and rain nourishes it,
And it serves men for fuel,
And he takes thereof and warms himself,
And he kindles *it* and bakes bread ;
Yea, he forms a god [an EL] and bows down,
He makes it an image and adores it.
Half of it he burns in fire,
With half of it he eats flesh ;
He roasts roast and is satisfied ;
He warms himself too, and says, ' Aha !
I am warm, I see a fire.'
But—*the* rest of it he makes into a god [an EL] into his image.
Adores it and bows down and prays to it,
And exclaims, ' Deliver me ; for thou art my EL !'

They have no knowledge and understand not ;

Chapter XLIV. 18—24.

For their eyes are smeared so that they cannot see,
Their hearts, that they cannot consider;
Neither does he take it to his heart,
Nor has he knowledge or sense to say,
Half of it have I burned in fire,
On its charcoal too have I baked bread,
Have roasted flesh and eaten :—
And shall I make its remnant an abomination ?
Shall I bow in worship to a tree-stock ?
He follows after ashes ;
A deceived heart has turned him aside,
So that he cannot deliver his soul, nor say,
Is there not a lie in my right hand ?

Remember these things, O Jacob,
And Israel, for thou art My servant :
I formed thee, thou art a servant to Me ;
O Israel, thou canst not be forgotten of Me.
I blot out thy rebellions as a cloud,
And as a mist thy sins :
Return to me, for I vindicate thee.
Rejoice, O Heavens, for Yahveh hath done *it*;
Shout, ye depths of earth !
Ye mountains, break forth into song,
Forest and every tree therein ;
For Yahveh liberates Jacob,
And will glorify himself in Israel !

Thus saith Yahveh, your liberator,
And He that formed thee from *the* womb

CHAPTERS XLIV. 24.—XLV. 3.

I am Yahveh who make all *things* ;
Stretching out *the* Heavens, alone,
Spreading forth the earth—who with Me ?—
Frustrating *the* signs of impostors,
And He makes diviners fools,—
Who turns wise men backwards,
And makes their knowledge folly ;
Who stablishes His servant's word,
And makes good *the* counsel of His messengers,
Who saith of Jerusalem, ' Let her be inhabited,'
And of Judah's cities, ' Let them be built,
And her wastes will I restore '—
Who saith of the Flood, ' Be thou wasted,
And thy streams will I dry up '—
Who saith of Cyrus, ' My shepherd !
And all My pleasures shall he accomplish '—
Who saith of Jerusalem, ' Let her be built,'
And of *the* temple, ' Let it be founded.'
Thus saith Yahveh, to his Anointed one, to Cyrus,
Whom I have held by his right hand,
To bring down nations before him,
And to ungird loins of kings,
To open folding-doors before him,
And that gateways may not be shut—
' I will go before thee, and will level heights ;
Folding-doors of brass will I break, and cleave bars of
   iron :
And I give thee treasures of darkness,
And hidden things of secret places,
That thou mayest know that I am Yahveh,

CHAPTER XLV. 3—10.

The God of Israel, who call thee by name.
It is for the sake of My servant Jacob and Israel Mine elect :
And I called unto thee by thy name,
I called thee by a title, though thou didst not know Me.
I am Yahveh and there is none else ;
Beside Me there is no Elohim.
I girded thee when thou hadst not known Me ;
That *men* may know from *the* rising of *the* sun
And from its setting, that there is none beside Me.
I am Yahveh and there is none else,
Forming light and creating darkness,
Making peace and creating evil ;
I, Yahveh, effect all these things.'

Shower, ye heavens, from above,
And let *the* skies pour down *God's* [EL] righteous dealing,
Let earth open, and *the heavens* bear fruit of deliverance,
And let righteous dealing spring up at once :
I, Yahveh, have created it.

Woe to him who strives with Him that formed him,
A potsherd of earth's potsherds !
Shall clay say to him who fashions it, What makest thou ?
Or thy work, ' He has no hands ? '
Woe to him who saith to a father, ' What begettest thou ? '
And to a woman, ' With what dost thou travail ? '

THE PROPHECIES OF ISAIAH.

CHAPTER XLV. 11—17.

Thus saith Yahveh, Israel's Holy One, and his fashioner,
Enquire ye of Me as to things to come—
Command ye Me concerning My sons and My handy work?
It was I who made *the* earth,
And created man upon it;
My hands stretched out *the* heavens,
And I gave charge to all their hosts:
It was I who raised him [Cyrus] up in righteous dealing,
And will make all his ways level:
He shall build My city and send forth My exiles,
Not for a price, and not for a reward;
Saith Yahveh Sabaoth.

Thus saith Yahveh:
Egypt's wealth and Æthiopia's gains,
And Sabeans, men of stature,
Shall pass over to thee and be thine,
Shall follow thee, pass over in chains,
And bow down to thee, supplicate thee:
'Surely,' *say they*, 'in thee is God, [EL, the Strong One],
And there is none beside—no Elohim!
Truly Thou art a mysterious God [EL],
Elohim of Israel, a deliverer.'
They are ashamed and confounded, all of them,—
Makers of idols go into confusion together:
Through Yahveh Israel is delivered with a lasting deliverance,—

Chapter XLV. 17—23.

Ye shall not blush nor come to shame for ever and ever.

For thus saith Yahveh who created the Heavens:
He is the Elohim who formed the earth and made it,
He established it—He did not create it *to be* a waste,
He formed it to be inhabited:
I am Yahveh, and there is none beside:
I have not spoken in secret,
In a place of a land of darkness:
I said not to *the* seed of Jacob, 'Seek ye •Me in vain;'
I am Yahveh who promise truly *and* announce uprightly.

Assemble yourselves, and come;
Approach together, ye escaped of the nations:
No knowledge have they who bear about their wooden idol,
And pray to a god who cannot deliver.
Declare ye, and bring *it* forth,
Yea, let them take counsel together:—
Who published this from ancient time—proclaimed it of old?
Was it not I, Yahveh, beside whom there is no Elohim?
A righteous EL and a Deliverer,
There is none beside Me!
Turn to Me and find deliverance,
All ye ends of earth,
For I am EL, and there is none else!
By Myself have I sworn,
From My mouth has a truth gone forth,
A word, and it shall not return,

CHAPTERS XLV. 23. XLVI. 6.

That to Me every knee shall bend,
Every tongue shall swear.
'Only in Yahveh'—one saith of Me—
'Have I righteous dealings and strength ; '
To him shall each one come, and ashamed shall they be,
All that were incensed against him ;
In Yahveh shall all *the* seed of Israel find righteous
    dealing and boast themselves.
Already Bel bows down—Nebo sinks—
Their images are *laid* on beast and cattle !
They whom ye carried are a load,
A burden to *the* weary *beast !*
They sink—they bow down together—
No power have they to rescue *the* burden
And they themselves go into captivity !

Hearken to Me, house of Jacob,
And all *the* remnant of *the* house of Israel !
The borne as a load from *the* belly,
The carried from *the* womb :
Even to old age am I the same,
And even to grey hairs will I carry :
I have made and I will bear,
And I will carry and will set free.

To whom will ye liken Me, and equal *Me*
And compare Me, that we may be like ?
They who pour out gold from *the* bag,
And weigh out silver in a balance,—

Chapter XLVI. 6.

They hire a metal-founder and he makes it a god [EL],
They fall down—aye, prostrate themselves :
They take it on shoulder and carry it,
And rest it in its place that it may stand,
That it remove not from its place :
Yea, one may cry to it, but it answers not,
Out of his trouble it saves not.

Remember this, and demean yourselves like men,
Take it to heart, ye rebellious ones :
Remember former things of old,
For I am EL, and there is none else,
—Elohim—and there is none like Me ;
Announcing *the* future from *the* first,
And from olden time, things yet undone,
Saying, My counsel shall stand,
And all My pleasure will I perform ;
Calling an eagle from *the* sunrise,
A man of My counsel from a distant land :
Yea, I said it, yea I will bring it to pass,
I purposed, yea I will accomplish it.
Hearken unto me, ye stubborn heart—
Ye that are far from righteous-dealing *with Me*—
I bring near My righteous-dealing—it is not distant,
And My deliverance shall tarry not ;
And in Zion do I appoint deliverance
And to Israel, My glory.

CHAPTERS XLVII. XLVIII.
The Doom of Babylon. Warnings to Israel. Promises of deliverance.

CHAPTER XLVII. 1—7.

Down, and sit on dust, O virgin daughter of Babylon!
Sit upon *the* ground without a throne, O daughter of Chaldea:
For not again shalt thou be called 'Tender and Delicate!'
Take millstones and grind meal:
Withdraw thy veil, uplift *the* skirt,
Bare *the* leg, wade *the* streams;
Let thy nakedness be laid bare,
Yea, let thy shame be seen.
'Revenge will I take,' *saith God* [EL], 'and spare no man:'
It is our Liberator; Yahveh Sabaoth His name,
Holy One of Israel!

Sit thou silent, and get thee into darkness, O daughter of Chaldea,
For not again shalt thou be called 'Mistress of Kingdoms.'
I was wroth with My people,
I profaned My heritage and gave them into thy hands:
Thou didst shew them no compassion,
Thou madest thy yoke press heavily on *the* aged,—
And thou saidst, I shall ever be a mistress;
So that thou didst not lay these *things* to thy heart,
Thou rememberedst not *the* latter end thereof.

Chapter XLVII. 8—13.

And now hear this, O voluptuous one,
Who sittest in security;
Who sayest in thy heart, ' I, and none beside ;
I shall not sit a widow,
Nor know the loss of children ; '
Yet in a moment, in one day, shall these two *things* befall thee,
Loss of children and widowhood ;
They shall come on thee in their completeness,
Amid thy many sorceries,
Amid *the* great multitude of thy spells.
For thou didst trust in thy wickedness—thou saidst,
  ' No one sees me '—
Thy wisdom and thy science, this perverted thee,
And thou saidst in thy heart, ' I, and none beside !'
Therefore an evil comes upon thee,
Which thou hast not skill to charm away ;*
And a mischief shall fall upon thee,
Which thou shalt not be able to appease,
And ruin, of which thou wast unaware,
Shall come suddenly upon thee !

Abide now in thy enchantments,
And in *the* multitude of thy sorceries,
In which thou has wearied thyself from thy youth up,—
Haply thou mayest profit by them,
Haply thou mayest strike terror !
Thou art self-wearied by thy many counsellings :
Let them now stand forth and rescue thee.

THE PROPHECIES OF ISAIAH.

Chapter XLVII. 13—XLVIII. 5.

(*The* dividers of the Heavens, the star gazers,
Prognosticators at new moons),
From things which shall come upon thee.
See—they are become as stubble,
A fire has burned them up,
They cannot rescue their life from hand of flame :—
It is not a coal to warm them,
Nor a fire to sit before!
Such are they become to thee about whom thou hast wearied thyself,
Traffickers with thee from thy youth :—
They have wandered off, every one to his quarter—
There is none to save thee!

Hear ye this, O house of Jacob,
The called by *the* name of Israel,
And who are come forth from Judah's fount,
Who swear by *the* name of Yahveh,
And confess *the* Elohim of Israel,
But not in truth, and not in sincerity,
Though they call themselves of the Holy City,
And stay themselves on *the* Elohim of Israel—
Yahveh Sabaoth His name!

I proclaimed the former things of old,
And from My mouth went they forth and I shewed them ;
I wrought *them* suddenly, and they came to pass.
Because I knew that thou *art* stubborn,
And thy neck a sinew of iron, and thy forehead brass,
Therefore I proclaimed it to thee of old,

Chapters XLVIII. 5—13.

Ere yet it came to pass, I made thee hear *it*;
Lest thou shouldest say, 'my idol hath done these *things*,
And my graven and my molten image commanded them.'
Thou hast heard—review it all:
And ye, will ye not declare it?
Henceforth I make thee hear new things,
Even hidden things, which thou knewest not;
Now are they created and not of old,
And before *this* day, and thou heardest not of them,
Lest thou shouldest say, 'Behold I knew them.'
Also thou heardest not, also thou knewest not,
Thine ear too was not opened of old;
For I knew that deceiving thou wouldest deceive,
And from *the* womb wast called 'Rebel':—
For My name's sake I defer Mine anger,
And *for* My praise I bridle myself toward thee,
That I might not cut thee off.
See! I refined thee—but not with *gain of* silver;
I tested thee in a furnace of distress;
For My own sake, for My own sake will I do *this*:
For how should *My name* be profaned!
And My glory I will not give to another.

Hearken to Me, O Jacob,
And Israel, My called one!
I am He: I first, I also last!
My hand also founded *the* earth,
And My right hand spread out *the* heavens

CHAPTER XLVIII. 13—21.

When I call to them, they stand forth together,
Assemble yourselves, all of you, and hearken :
Who amongst them has announced these things ?
' He whom Yahveh loves will accomplish his pleasure on Babylon,
And his arm *shall be upon the* Chaldeans ? '
I, I have spoken ; I also have summoned him,
I have brought him, and his way shall prosper.

Draw near to Me—hear ye this.
Not in secret spake I from the first,
From the time that *the purpose* was, there was I,
And now Adonai Yahveh hath sent me, and His Spirit.
Thus saith Yahveh thy Liberator, Israel's Holy One :
I am Yahveh, thine Elohim, who teach thee to prosper,
Leading thee by *the* way thou shouldest go :—
If thou heedest My bidding,
Then shall thy welfare be as a stream,
And thy prosperity as waves of the sea,
And thy seed shall be as *the* sea-sand,
And issue of thy bowels as its bowels : *
His name shall not be cut off nor destroyed from before Me.

Go ye forth from Babel : flee from Chaldea :
With voice of joy declare it and make it heard,
Cause it to go forth to *the* end of the earth :
Say ye, ' Yahveh hath set free his servant Jacob,
And they thirsted not in deserts *through which* he led them,

Chapter XLVIII. 21.—XLIX. 5.

He caused waters to flow for them from a rock,
He clave a rock also, and waters burst forth :'—
But there is no welfare, saith Yahveh, for *the* unrighteous.

CHAPTER XLIX.

An Address by the Prophet as " Servant of God" (who in v. 3 is called Israel, as the representative of the people), to the faithful remnant in Israel.

Hearken to me, ye countries,
And attend, ye far off peoples !
From *the* womb has Yahveh called me,
From my mother's bowels has He mentioned my name :
And He has made my mouth like a sharp sword,
In *the* shadow of His hand has He hidden me ;
And He has made me a polished arrow,
In His quiver has He covered me :
And He said to me, ' My servant thou, O Israel,
By whom I will glorify myself.'
Then said I, ' I have toiled in vain,
For nought and vanity have I spent my strength ;
Yet with Yahveh is my cause,
And my recompence with my Elohim.'
And now Yahveh saith,
He who formed me from *the* womb to be a servant to Him,
To restore Jacob unto Him,
And that Israel may be gathered to Him ;
—For in *the* eyes of Yahveh am I honoured,

CHAPTER XLIX. 5—10.

And my Elohim is become my strength—
And he said, Too light a thing is it that thou shouldest be
   My servant,
To restore the tribes of Jacob,
And to bring back *the* preserved of Israel :
I also appoint thee as a light of nations,
That My deliverance may be to *the* end of the earth.

Thus saith Yahveh,
The Liberator of Israel, his Holy One,
To him whose life is despised,
To *the* abhorred of *the* nation,
To a servant of tyrants :
Kings shall behold and they arise,
Princes, and they shall make obeisance,
Because of Yahveh who is faithful,
Israel's Holy One, for He chose thee.
Thus saith Yahveh :
In a time of favour do I answer thee,
And in a day of deliverance I help thee ;
And I preserve thee and appoint thee for a covenant of
   the people,
To set up *the* land,
To cause waste heritages to be inherited,
Saying to captives, ' Go forth ; '
To those in darkness, ' Shew yourselves : '—
On pathways shall they feed,
And on all bare-hills *shall be* their pasturage :
They shall not hunger and they shall not thirst,
And mirage and sun shall not smite them,

Chapter XLIX. 10—19.

For He that compassionates them will lead them,
And to water-springs will guide them.
And I make all My mountains a road,
And My highways shall be raised.
See! these come from afar;
And see! those from North and from West,
And those from *the* land of *the* Sinim!
Shout O heavens, and rejoice O earth!
Break forth into song, O mountains!
For Yahveh comforts His people,
And has compassion upon His afflicted.

Yet, saith Zion, 'Yahveh has forsaken me,
And Adonai has forgotten me:'—
But will a woman *so* forget her suckling,
As to have no tenderness for *the* son of her womb?
Even these may forget,
But I will not forget thee!
See! on *the* palms of *My* hands have I graven thee—
Thy walls *are* ever before Me,—
Thy children are hastening forth to *thee*,*—
And thy destroyers and thy wasters depart from thee!
Lift up thine eyes around, and look:
They are all assembled—are come to thee.
As I live—*it is* Yahveh's utterance—
Thou shalt surely clothe thee with them all as with an ornament,
And bind them on thee, like a bride.
Surely, as for thy wastes and thy desolations and thy ruined land—

CHAPTER XLIX. 19—25.

Yea, now wilt thou be too strait for *the* inhabitants,
And they who swallowed thee up shall be far away !
The sons of thy bereavement shall yet say in thine ears,
' The place is narrow for me ;
Move away for me that I may dwell ; '
So that thou sayest in thine heart,
' Who hath begotten me these,
For I was bereaved and barren,
Exiled and outcast ?
And these, who reared them ?
Behold I was left alone,
These—where *have* they *been !* '

Thus saith Adonai Yahveh :
See ! I will lift up my hand to nations,
And hoist my banner to peoples,
And they shall bring thy sons in *their* bosom,
And thy daughters shall be borne on shoulder,
And kings will be thy foster-fathers,
And their princesses thy nursing-mothers :
Face on ground shall they do thee homage,
And lick *the* dust of thy feet,
And thou shalt know that I am Yahveh,
I, in whom they that hope shall not be ashamed.

Is booty to be snatched away from a hero ?
Or, can righteous captives be rescued ?
For thus saith Yahveh :
Even a hero's captives can be snatched away,
And a terrible man's booty be rescued :

CHAPTER XLIX. 25—L. 3.

For I will contend with him who contends with thee,
And thy children will I deliver;
And I will feed their oppressors with their own flesh,
And *with* their own blood, as *with* new wine, shall they be drunken,
And all flesh shall know,
That I am Yahveh thy Deliverer,
And thy Liberator, Jacob's Mighty One.

CHAPTERS L.

The bond between Yahveh and Israel not broken by divorce or sale. Their sole trust must be in Him.

Thus saith Yahveh:
Where is the bill of your mother's divorce, with which I put her away?
Or, which of my creditors *is it* to whom I sold you?
Lo! for your iniquities were ye sold,
And for your transgressions was your mother put away!
Wherefore when I came, was there no man—
When I called was there none to answer?
Is My hand too short to redeem,
And is there no power in Me to deliver?
Lo! with My rebuke I dry up a sea,
I make rivers a desert—
Their fish stink for lack of water,
And die for thirst—
I clothe *the* heavens *in* mourning,

CHAPTER L. 3—10.

And sackcloth I make their mantle.

Adonai Yahveh has given me *the* tongue of *His* taught ones,
That I might know how to refresh the weary with counsel :
He wakens morn by morn, wakens Mine ear,
To hearken as taught ones *hearken :*
Adonai Yahveh hath opened Mine ear,
And I have not been rebellious,
I have not turned backward.
My back I gave to smiters,
And My cheeks to pluckers *of the beard*—
My face I hid not from shame and spitting.
But Adonai Yahveh will help Me,
Therefore am I not confounded :
Therefore have I set My face like a flint,
And I know that I shall not be ashamed.
My justifier is near :—
Who will contend with Me ? let us stand forth together :
Who is My opponent ? let him draw near to Me.
Lo, Adonai Yahveh will help Me ;
Who is he that can worst Me ?
Lo, they will all decay like a garment—
The moth will devour them.

Who among you fears Yahveh,
Hearkening to *the* voice of his servant,
Who *yet* walks in darknesses and has no light ?
Let him trust in *the* name of Yahveh,

Chapter L. 10—LI. 3.

And lean upon his Elohim.
See, all of ye, kindlers of a fire, girt round with fire brands,—
Begone unto *the* flame of your own fire,
And unto *the* firebrands ye have lighted!
From my hand this befalls *you*;
Ye shall lie down in torment.

CHAPTERS LI. LII.

Promises of a near deliverance to the nation, prostrate beneath the Babylonian yoke.

Chapters LI. 1.

Hear me, ye followers of righteous dealing,
Ye that seek Yahveh:
Look to *the* rock *whence* ye were hewn,
And to *the* pit-quarry *whence* ye were digged:
Look to Abraham your father,
And to Sarah who bare you,
How I called him *when* but one,
And blessed him and multiplied him!
For Yahveh comforts Zion,
Comforts all her ruins,
And makes her wilderness like Eden,
And her desert like a garden of Yahveh:
Joy and gladness shall be found in her,
Praise and voice of song.

CHAPTER LI. 4—9.

Attend to Me, My people !
And give ear to Me, My nation !
For instruction shall proceed from Me,
And my law will I stablish
For a light of peoples.
Near is My righteous-dealing—My deliverance is gone forth—
And My arms will judge peoples ;
And for Me *the* countries shall long,
And for My arm shall wait.

Lift up your eyes to *the* heavens,
And look upon the earth beneath ;
For *the* heavens shall pass away like smoke,
And the earth fall to pieces like a garment,
And its inhabitants die like a gnat ;
But My deliverance shall be for ever,
And My righteous-dealing shall not be broken down.
Hearken to Me, ye who know *My* righteous-dealing,
The people in whose heart is My teaching ;
Fear ye not frail-man's reproach,
Nor be broken down at their revilings ;
For *the* moth will eat them like a garment,
And *the* worm will eat them like wool,
But My just-dealing will be for ever,
And My deliverance to all generations.

Awake, awake, arm of Yahveh ! clothe thee with might !
Awake as *in* ancient days, *in* generations of old !
Art not thou it that didst cleave Rahab

CHAPTER LI. 9—16.

And pierce *the* sea-monster?
Art thou not it that driedst up a sea,
Waters of a mighty deep—
That made sea-deeps a way
For *the* liberated to pass over?
And *the* freed-men of Yahveh shall return,
And with shouting come to Zion,
With everlasting joy upon their head;
Joy and gladness shall they obtain—
Sorrow and sighing flee away.

I, I am He, your comforter:
Who art thou, that thou fearest a frail-man that dieth,
And a son of man *who* is given up *to the mower as grass*;
And didst forget Yahveh thy maker,
Who stretched forth heaven and founded earth,
And fearedst alway all the day,
Because of the oppressor's fury,
When ready to destroy?
Yet where is the oppressor's fury?
He that is bowed down will soon be freed,
And will not die for *the* pit,
Neither will his bread fail:
For I am Yahveh thine Elohim,
Who stir the sea so that its billows roar,
Yahveh Sabaoth His name!
And I put My words in thy mouth,
And in *the* shadow of My hand I cover thee,
That I may plant *the* heavens and found *the* earth,

CHAPTER LI. 16—23.
And say to Zion, ' My people Thou.'

Arouse thee ! arouse thee ! stand up, O Jerusalem !
Thou who hast drunk from Yahveh's hand the cup of
   His wrath,
Hast drunk—hast drained—the goblet-cup of stagger-
   ing !
None was there to guide her of all *the* sons she had
   borne,
And none, of all *the* sons she *had reared*, to grasp her
   by *the* hand,
These two things befell thee—
Who is there to condole with thee ?—
The desolation and the destruction,
And the famine and the sword !
In what guise shall I comfort thee ?
Thy sons faint—they lie at *the* head of all streets,
Like a netted antelope ;
Full of Yahveh's fury, of *the* rebuke of thine Elohim.
Therefore hear now this, O afflicted one,
And drunken, but not with wine :
Thus saith thy Lord Yahveh,
And thine Elohim who pleadeth for his people,
' Lo, I take out of thy hand the cup of staggering,
The goblet-cup of My wrath—
Not again shalt thou drink it—
And I place it in *the* hand of those who oppressed thee,
Who said to thy soul, Bow down that we may pass
   over ;
And thou madest thy back as *the* ground,

CHAPTERS LI. 23.—LII. 7.

And as a street for passengers.'

Awake, awake! put on thy strength, O Zion!
Put on thy splendid garments, Jerusalem, the holy city!
For *the* uncircumcised and unclean shall enter thee no
 more.
Shake thyself from *the* dust, arise, take thy seat, O
 Jerusalem;
Loose thyself from *the* bonds of thy neck,
O captive daughter of Zion!
For thus saith Yahveh:
For nought were ye sold,
But not with money shall ye be bought back.
Thus saith Adonai Yahveh:
My people went down into Egypt at *the* beginning
 there to sojourn,
And Asshur, without cause, oppressed him;
And now what have I here?—*it is* an utterance of
 Yahveh—
For My people has been taken away for nought?
His rulers shout *over them*—*it is* an utterance of
 Yahveh—
And ever, all the day, is My name reviled.
Therefore shall My people know My name—
Therefore in that day *they shall know*
That I am He who said, 'Here am I.'

How beautiful upon the mountains a herald's feet!
Announcer of peace—herald of good—announcer of
 deliverance—

THE PROPHECIES OF ISAIAH. 139

CHAPTER LII. 7—14.

Who saith to Zion, ' Thine Elohim reigns ! '
It is thy watchmen's voice ! *their* voice they uplift ;
With accord they shout,
For they behold eye to eye
The return of Yahveh to Zion !
Break forth and shout together, ye ruins of Jerusalem,
For Yahveh comforts His people, redeems Jerusalem !
Yahveh lays bare His holy arm in *the* eyes of all the nations,
And all ends of earth behold the deliverance of our Elohim,
' Depart ye—depart ye—go out thence—
Touch not an unclean thing—
Go ye out from her midst,
Keep yourselves pure, ye bearers of Yahveh's vessels ' :
For not in haste shall ye go forth,
Nor proceed in flight,
For at your front proceeds Yahveh,
And Israel's Elohim brings up your rear,

CHAPTERS LII. 13. LIII.

Vicarious atonement. The servant of Yahveh victorious through suffering endured for others.

Behold, my servant shall prosper,
Shall be high, and uplifted, and very lofty !
As, many were amazed at thee

Chapters LII. 14—LIII. 6.

—So marred His aspect beyond that of man,
And His form beyond that of sons of men—
So shall He cause many nations to start up:
Kings will shut their mouths because of Him,
Because they see what had not been told them,
And perceive what they had not heard.

Who believed our tidings?
And Yahveh's arm—to whom was it made manifest?
For as a tender shoot He grew up before Him,
And as a root out of a parched ground:
He had no grace nor splendour that we should regard Him,
Nor aspect that we should delight in Him:—
Despised and forsaken of men,
A man of pains and acquainted with sickness,
And like one from whom men hide *their* face!
Despised, and we esteemed Him not!

But surely He bore our sicknesses,
And our sufferings—He carried them;
Whilst we esteemed Him smitten,
Stricken of Elohim, and afflicted,
Yet was He pierced through our rebellions,
Bruised through our misdeeds:
A chastisement, *to* our welfare, was upon Him.
And we, by His stripes, are healed.
Like sheep we all had gone astray,
We turned every one to his own way,
And Yahveh made the guilt of us all to light on Him.

CHAPTER LIII. 7.

He was oppressed, yet He submitted himself,
And opened not His mouth;
As a sheep that is led to slaughter,
And as an ewe that is dumb before her shearers;
And opened not His mouth.
Through oppression and through a judgment was He taken off—
Yet, of his generation who considered
That He was cut off out of *the* land of *the* living,
That for *the* rebellion of my people He was stricken?
And His sepulchre was appointed with *the* wicked,*
And His grave-mound with *the* oppressor,
Although He had done no injustice,
Neither was deceit in His mouth.
Yet did it please Yahveh to bruise Him—He made Him sick:—
If Thou make His soul a sin-offering,
He would see a seed, would prolong *His* days,
And Yahveh's purpose would prosper in His hand:
Free from travail of His soul He would see *and* be satisfied;
By His knowledge would My righteous servant make many righteous,
And of their iniquities He would bear the burden.
Therefore will I assign Him a portion among the great,
And with the strong shall He divide spoil,
Because He poured out His soul unto death,
And was numbered with transgressors,
Though *it was* He *who* had borne *the* sin of many,
And had interceded for *the* rebellious.

CHAPTERS LIV.—LVII.

Encouragements to returning Israel. Warnings against religious defection.

CHAPTER LIV. 1—7.

Shout, O barren one, *who* hast not borne!
Break forth into shouting and exult, thou that travailedst
    not!
For more are *the* children of *the* desolate,
Than *the* children of *the* married woman, saith Yahveh.
Widen *the* place of thy tent,
And let them stretch forth *the* curtains of thy dwelling:
Hold not back—lengthen thy tent-cords,
And firmly fix thy tent-pins,
For, right and left, shalt thou burst forth,
And thy seed will inherit nations,
And ruined cities will they people.
Fear not, for thou shall not be shamed;
And be not confounded, for thou wilt not be brought to
    reproach:
Yea, *the* shame of thy maidenhood shalt thou forget,
And no more remember the reproach of thy widowhood;
For thy maker is thy husband,
Yahveh Sabaoth His name,
And thy Vindicator Israel's Holy One,
Elohim of the whole earth is He called.
For as a woman rejected and dejected* did Yahveh call
    thee,
And as a wife of youth:—that she should be despised!—
Saith thine Elohim.
For a little moment did I reject thee,
But with great compassions will I gather thee:

CHAPTER LIV. 8—16.

In an outpouring of wrath,* I hid my face from thee a moment,
But with lasting kindness I compassionate thee,
Saith Yahveh, thy Vindicator.

For with Me, this *is* as *the* waters of Noah :
As I have sworn that *the* waters of Noah should no more overpass the earth,
So have I sworn not to be wroth with thee, nor rebuke thee :
Though the mountains should depart and the hills remove,
Yet from thee My kindness shall not depart,
And *the* covenant of My peace shall not remove,
Saith He who hath compassion on thee, Yahveh.
O afflicted one, storm-tossed, unconsoled !
Behold, I set thy stones in paint-cement,
And with sapphires lay thy foundations ;
And I make thy battlements into rubies,
And thy gates into carbuncle-stones,
And all thy boundaries into stones of price ;
And all thy sons are disciples of Yahveh ;
And great *the* welfare of thy children :
By *My* righteous dealing *with thee* shalt thou be stablished.
Be far from *thought of* oppression, for thou needest not fear,
And from alarm, for it shall not approach thee :—
See ! if *any* gather together, it is not of Me :
Whoso musters against thee, shall fall away unto thee !
See ! it was I who made *the* smith,

CHAPTERS LIV. 16.—LV. 6.

Who blows upon a fire of charcoal,
And brings forth a weapon as his work,
And it was I who made a spoiler to lay waste
But no weapon formed against thee shall succeed,
And every tongue that rises for judgment against thee
    shalt thou worst.
This is a heritage of Yahveh's servants,
And their justification that is from Me :
It is an utterance of Yahveh.
Hah ! every thirsty one ! come ye to waters,
And he who has no money—come ye, buy and eat :
And come, buy wine and milk,
Without money and without price.
Why weigh out money for that which is not bread ?
And your gains for that which is not unto satiety ?
Hearken ye, hearken to me and eat *the* good,
And let your soul revel in fatness :
Incline your ear and come to me,
Hearken, and your soul shall revive,
And I will make with you a lasting covenant,
Mercies *like those* of David,—the unfailing ones.
See ! I have made him a witness to peoples—
A leader and commander of peoples !
Lo ! thou wilt call a nation thou knewest not,
And nations which knew thee not will run to thee,
Because of Yahveh your Elohim,
And for Israel's Holy One, for He hath made thee
    glorious.

Seek ye Yahveh while He may be found,

CHAPTER LV. 6.

Call ye on Him while He is near ;
Let *the* wicked man forsake his way,
And a man of sin his thoughts,
And let him return to Yahveh, and He will have mercy upon him,
And to our Elohim, for He will abundantly pardon.
For My thoughts are not your thoughts,
Neither are your ways My ways :—an oracle of Yahveh ;
For Heaven is higher than earth ;
So are My ways higher than your ways,
And My thoughts than your thoughts.
For as the rain comes down, and the snow from the heavens,
And returns not thither, except it hath watered the earth,
And made it bring forth and bud,
And given seed to sower and bread to eater :
So shall My word which goes forth from My mouth,
It shall not return to Me void,
Except it hath effected what I please,
And prospered that for which I sent it.
For with joy shall ye go forth,
And with peace be led along :
The mountains and hills shall break forth before you into shouting,
And all trees of the field shall clap *the* hand :
Instead of the thorn shall come up cypress,
And instead of the nettle shall come up myrtle,
And it shall be to Yahveh for a name,
For a lasting sign :—*it* shall not be cut off.

Chapters LVI. 1—7.

Thus saith Yahveh :
Keep to justice, and practise righteous-dealing,
For My deliverance is near to come,
And My righteous-dealing to be made manifest,
Happy a mortal-man who does this,
And a son of man who lays hold thereon ;
Keeping Sabbath that he profane it not,
And keeping his hand that it do no evil.
And let not a son of the alien speak—
He that has joined himself to Yahveh—saying,
'Yahveh will surely sever me from his people.'
Nor let the eunuch say, 'Lo, I am a dry tree.'
For thus saith Yahveh of eunuchs who keep my Sabbaths,
And choose what I delight in and lay hold on My covenant,
'To them give I within My house and within My walls,
A memorial and a name better than of sons and daughters ;
A lasting name will I give them which shall not be cut off,
And sons of the alien who join themselves to Yahveh,
To minister to Him—to love the name of Yahveh,—
To become His servants—
Every one keeping Sabbath so that he profane it not,
And those who lay hold on My covenant :—
Them bring I to My holy hill,
And gladden them in My house of prayer :
Their burnt offerings and sacrifices
Shall be for acceptance upon My altar,
For My house shall be called a house of prayer for all the peoples—'

CHAPTER LVI. 8.—LVII. 4.

An oracle of Adonai Yahveh,
Who gathers *the* outcasts of Israel
' To his gathered ones I yet will gather unto him.'

Come, all ye beasts of *the* field,
All ye beasts in *the* forest, to devour !
His watchmen are blind, all of them without knowledge !
Dumb dogs, all of them—they have no power to bark—
Seers that lie down, loving to slumber—
And the dogs are mighty of appetite,—
They know not how to be satisfied !
And these are shepherds who know not discretion ;
They turn all of them to their own way,
Each one, without exception, after his gain.
Come,' *say they*, ' let me fetch wine,
And let us quaff strong drink ;
And to-morrow shall be as this day,
Great—far surpassing.'

The righteous perishes, and no man lays it to heart ;
And pious men are taken away, while no one considers
That the righteous is taken away because of the evil :—
He enters into peace !
They rest upon their beds—
Whoso walked *in* his *own* straight *path !*
But ye ! draw nigh hither ye sons of a sorceress,
Seed of an adulterer, and *thyself* a harlot !
Against whom do ye disport yourselves ?
Against whom do ye widen mouth and stretch out
 tongue ?

Chapter LVII. 4—11.

Are ye not a rebel offspring, a seed of falsehood—
The enflamed with gods under every green tree,
Slaughterers of the children in torrent-beds,
Beneath clefts of the rocks?
Thy portion is with smooth stones of a torrent-bed *—
These, these are thy lot—
Even to these hast thou poured drink-offerings,
Presented meal-offerings!
With these *things* can I quiet Myself?

On a lofty and upraised mountain hast thou placed thy bed;
And thither hast thou gone up to offer sacrifice,
And hast placed thy memorial behind the door and the post
For to other than Me thou uncoveredst and wentest up,
Didst enlarge thy bed, and madest thy terms with them;
Lovedst their bed—lookedst out a place—
Didst wander also to Moloch with unguent,
And didst multiply thy perfumes,
And didst send thy messengers afar,
And didst debase thyself to Sheol :—
Thou wast wearied by the length of thy way,
But saidst not, '*It is* hopeless':
Thou didst find vigour to thy hand,
Wherefore thou wast not exhausted.
But of whom hast thou been fearful—
And afraid—that thou hast dealt falsely
And hast not remembered Me, hast not taken *it* to thy heart?

CHAPTER LVII. 11—18.

Is it not that I have been silent, even from of old?
Therefore thou fearedst Me not.
I announce My righteous dealing with thee;
But as for your workmanship—they will not avail thee;
When thou criest *for help*, let thy throng *of deities* deliver thee!
But a blast shall take all of them away,
A breath shall bear them off:
But he that trusteth in Me shall inherit *the* land,
And take possession of My holy hill.

And *a voice* said, 'Cast ye up, cast ye up, prepare a way;
Remove stumbling blocks from My people's way.'
For thus saith He who is high and exalted,
Abiding eternally, and whose name is Holy One;
On high and *in the* sanctuary I dwell,
With him also who is crushed and lowly of spirit,
To revive the spirit of *the* lowly,
And to revive *the* heart of *the* crushed.
For not alway will I contend,
Nor will I be for ever wroth,
Else would the spirit faint before Me,
And souls which I have made.
For *the* guilt of his greed was I wroth and smote him,
—Hiding Myself—and I was wroth,—
But turning aside, he went on in *the* way of his own heart.

'I saw his ways; but I will heal him, and lead him,
And him and his mourners will I requite with comforts,

Chapter LVII. 19.—LVIII. 4.

Creating *the* fruit of *the* lips ;
Peace, peace, to *the* distant and to *the* near,'
—Saith Yahveh—' And I will heal him,'
But the wicked are like a troubled sea,
For it cannot rest,
And its waters toss up mire and dirt.
' No peace,' saith mine Elohim, ' for *the* wicked.'

CHAPTERS LVIII. LIX.

Exhortations to sincerity, true Fasts, Sabbath observance: notwithstanding the sins of the people, Yahveh will effect deliverance.

' Cry with *deep* throat—refrain not—
Like a trumpet uplift thy voice,
And proclaim to My people their rebellion,
And to *the* house of Jacob their sins.'
And *yet* they enquire of Me daily,
And desire a knowledge of My ways,
As a nation that had done righteousness,
And had not forsaken *the* ordinance of its Elohim :
They ask of Me ordanances of *My* righteous-dealing,
They desire an approach of Elohim:—
' Why have we fasted, and Thou regardest not—
Humbled our soul, and Thou takest no knowledge ?'
Ah ! on your fast day ye follow business
And enforce all your tasks !
Ah ! ye fast for strife and contention,

Chapter LVIII. 4—11.

And to smite with fist of wickedness!
Ye fast not now so as to make your voice be heard on high.
Is this such a fast as I would choose,
A day when a man should humble his soul?
Is it to hang his head like a bulrush,
And to make sackcloth and ashes his couch?
Callest thou this a fast and a day acceptable to Yahveh?
Is not this the fast that I choose—
To loosen bands of wickedness,
To untie fastenings of *the* yoke,
And send forth *the* oppressed free,
And that ye burst asunder every yoke?
Is it not to break thy bread to *the* famishing,
And to bring home miserable outcasts,—
When thou seest a naked man, that thou clothe him,
And not hide thyself from thine own flesh?
Then as *the* dawn shall thy light break forth,
And thy healing shall spring up speedily;
My rightous-dealing with thee shall go before thee,
Yahveh's glory will bring up thy rear.
Then shalt thou call and Yahveh answer,
Thou shalt cry, and 'Here am I' will He say.
If from thy midst thou remoke *the* yoke,
Pointed finger and evil speech;
And if thou lavish thy self on *the* famishing
And satisfy *the* afflicted soul,
Then thy light beams forth in darkness,
And thy darkness *is* as mid-day;
And Yahveh always leads thee,

Chapter LVIII. 11—LIX. 3.

And satisfies thy soul in droughts,
And will strengthen thy bones ;
And thou becomest like a richly watered garden,
And like a spring of waters, whose waters will not deceive,
And they *that are* of thee, rebuild *the* ancient ruins,
Foundations of past generations—thou rearest *them* again—
And men shall call thee, Repairer of a Breach,
Restorer of paths, to dwell in.

If thou turn back thy foot from *the* Sabbath,
From doing thy business on My holy day,
And call *the* Sabbath a delight,
The holy of Yahveh, honourable ;
And if thou honour it, so as to refrain from thy ways,
Not pursuing thy business and talking *idle* talk,
Then shalt thou delight thyself in Yahveh,
And I will make thee ride over *the* heights of *the* land,
And feed thee with *the* inheritance of thy father Jacob :
For *the* mouth of Yahveh has spoken *it*.

Behold ! *the* hand of Yahveh is not too short to deliver,
Nor His ear too heavy to hearken ;
But your iniquities have separated between you and your Elohim,
And your sins have hidden *His* face from you that He hears not.
For with blood are your hands defiled
And your fingers with iniquity ;
Your lips speak falsehood,

CHAPTER LIX. 3—10.

Your tongue mutters perverseness.
No one pleads with uprightness,
And no one judges in faithfulness,
—Trusting in vanity and speaking falsehood,
Conceiving mischief and bringing forth iniquity.
Eggs of basilisk do they hatch,
And webs of spider do they weave;
He who eats of their eggs will die,
And the crushed one breaks out a viper:
Not for clothing serve their webs,
Nor can men cover themselves with their works:
Their works are works of mischief,
And in their hands *is the* deed of violence.
Their feet run to wickedness,
And hasten to shed innocent blood:
Their thoughts, thoughts of mischief,
Ruin and destruction in their highways:*
Way of peace they know not
And in their tracks is no judgment
Their paths have they made crooked for themselves,
Everyone walking thereon knows not peace.

Therefore has judgment been far from us,
And *God's* faithful dealing reaches us not:
We wait for light, but behold darkness,
For sunshine, *but* we walk in glooms:
Like blind *persons*, we grope along a wall,
And like *the* eyeless we grope—
We stumble at midday as in twilight,
We are like dead men among the healthy:

CHAPTER LIX. 11—18.

We murmur, all of us, like bears,
And like doves moaning we moan :
We wait for judgment but there is none,
For deliverance, but it is far from us.
Yea, our rebellions are many before Thee,
And our misdoings witness against us ;
Yea, our rebellions are with us,
And as for our iniquities, we are conscious of them ;--
Rebellion and denial of Yahveh,
And drawing back from after our Elohim ;—
Conceiving and uttering from *the* heart words of falsehood.
Therefore was judgment turned back
And *God's* faithful dealing stood afar off ;
For truth has stumbled in *the* street,
And uprightness cannot enter ;
And the truth is lacking,
And he that shuns evil makes himself a prey.
And Yahveh beheld :—
And ill seemed it in His eyes that there was no judgment ;
And He saw that there was no one,
And was astonished that there was none to interpose ;
So His own arm wrought out deliverance for Him,
And His righteous-dealing sustained Him :
And He put on righteous-dealing as mail,
And a helm of deliverance on His head ;
And for clothing He clothed himself in garments of revenge,
And clad Himself with jealousy as with a war-cloke :—
According to their deserts, so will He repay,

CHAPTER LIX. 18.—LX 2.

Wrath to His foes, requital to His enemies,
To *the* countries will He render requital :
And from *the* sunset shall they fear the name of Yahveh,
And from *the* sunrise His glory ;
For it will come like a pent up river,
Which Yahveh's breath drives on ;
But to Zion He comes a Vindicator,
And to those in Jacob who turn from rebellion :—
An utterance of Yahveh.

And as for Me, this is My covenant with them, saith
    Yahveh ;
My spirit which is upon thee,
And My words which I have put in thy mouth,
From thy mouth shall not depart,
Nor from *the* mouth of thy seed,
Nor from *the* mouth of thy seed's seed, saith Yahveh,—
From henceforth and for ever.

CHAPTER LX. 1—7.

*Address to the prostrate Jewish Church and nation, with
promises of return to the exiles : The rebuilding of the
Temple and the splendour of the restored Jerusalem.*

Arise—give forth light—for thy light has come—
And Yahveh's glory has dawned upon thee !
For lo ! darkness covers *the* earth,
And cloud-gloom *the* peoples ;

CHAPTER LX. 2—9.

But Yahveh dawns on thee ;
And His glory is seen upon thee ;
And nations come to thy light,
And kings to *the* brightness of thy dawning.
Lift up thine eyes around and see :
All of them are gathered together—to thee they come :
From afar thy sons come,
And at *the* side are thy daughters borne.

Then shall thou see and brighten up ;
And thy heart shall throb and swell,
For to thee shall turn *the* riches of *the* sea,
And the wealth of nations come to thee
An abundance of camels shall cover thee—
Young camels of Midian and Ephah ;
From Sheba shall they come, all of them,
Shall bear gold and incense,
And proclaim *the* praises of Yahveh.
To thee shall gather all *the* flocks of Kedar,
Nebaioth's rams shall serve thee ;
With acceptance shall they mount My altar,
And the house of My glory will I glorify,
Who are these that fly like a cloud,
And like doves to their cotes ?
Yea, *the* countries await Me,
And ships of Tarshish, foremost,
To bring thy sons from far,
Their silver and their gold with them,
For *the* name of Yahveh your Elohim,
And for Israel's Holy One, because He glorifies thee.

CHAPTER LX. 10—17.

And sons of *the* alien shall build up thy walls *
And their kings do thee service :
For in My wroth I smote thee,
But in My favour I have compassion on thee :
And thy gates shall be always open,
Day and night shall they be unshut,
That men may bring *the* wealth of nations to thee,
And their kings led *as captives*.
For the nation and the kingdom which will not serve thee shall perish,
Yea, the nations shall be utterly desolated,
The glory of the Lebanon shall come to thee,
Cypress, plane and cedar together,
To adorn *the* place of My sanctuary,
And *the* place of My feet will I make glorious :
Sons also of thine oppressors go crouching to thee,
And all that scorned thee do homage at *the* soles of thy feet,
And they call thee 'City of Yahveh,
Zion of *the* Holy One of Israel.'
Instead of thy being forsaken and hated,
And none passing through *thee*,
I even make thee a lasting pride,
A delight of generation and generation ;
And thou shalt suck *the* milk of nations,
And suck *the* breast of kings,
And know that I Yahveh am thy Deliverer,
And that thy Vindicator is the Strong one of Jacob.
Instead of copper will I bring gold,
And instead of the iron will I bring silver,

CHAPTER LX 17.

And copper instead of the wood,
And instead of the stones, iron ;
And I make thy peace thy government,
And thy rulers righteousness :
No more shall violence be heard of in thy land,
Ruin and destruction in thy borders,
But thou shalt call thy walls, ' Deliverance,'
And thy gates ' Praise.'

No more shall the sun be thy light by day,
Nor the moon shine on thee for brightness,
But Yahveh shall be to thee for a lasting light,
And thine Elohim thy glory.
Thy sun shall set no more,
And thy moon shall not wane,
For Yahveh shall be to thee for a lasting light,
And *the* days of thy mourning come to an end.
And thy people, all of them, *are* righteous,
They shall ever possess *the* land ;
A branch of My planting,
A work of My hand, to get Me glory.
The little one shall become a thousand,
And the small, a mighty nation :
I, Yahveh, will hasten it in its time.

CHAPTERS LXI. LXII.

The 'servant' of Yahveh (who is the speaker throughout these chapters), describes the message of favour, and of consequent prosperity, entrusted to him for Israel.

CHAPTERS LXI. 1—6.

The spirit of Adonai Yahveh is upon me ;
For Yahveh has anointed me,
To announce good tidings to the afflicted ;
To bind up *the* broken of heart hath he sent *me*,
To proclaim freedom to captives.
And opening *of prison* to bondsmen ;
To proclaim a year of grace for Yahveh,
And a day of vengeance for our Elohim ;
To comfort all mourners,
To appoint to Zion's mourners,
Instead of ashes to give them a coronal,*
Oil of joy instead of mourning,
Instead of a fainting spirit a garment of praise,
That men may call them 'Terebinths of *God's* righteous dealings,'
The planting of Yahveh that He may get Him glory.

Then build they up *the* ancient ruins,
They uprear desolations of *the* forefathers,
And they renew ruined cities,
Desolations of many generations :
And strangers stand and feed your flocks,
And aliens are your plowmen and vinedressers,
But ye—priests of Yahveh shall ye be called ;
Ministers of our Elohim shall ye be named.

Chapter LXI. 6—LXII. 1.

Riches of nations shall ye consume,
And to their splendour will ye succeed;
In place of your shame *shall ye receive* twofold,
And *in place of* contumely they shall exalt *in* their lot;
Therefore in their *own* land will they inherit twofold,—
Theirs shall be a lasting joy.
For I, Yahveh, love judgment,
Rapine with wrong I hate,
Therefore I give them their reward in faithfulness,
And make with them a lasting covenant,
So that their seed shall be famous among *the* nations,
And their offspring in *the* midst of the peoples;
All that see them shall own of them,
That they are a seed whom Yahveh has blessed.

With joy will I rejoice in Yahveh:
Let my soul rejoice in my Elohim,
For He has clothed me with garments of deliverance,
In a mantle of righteous-*dealing* He has wrapped me;
Like a bridegroom who wears a priest-like coronal,
And like a bride who decks herself with her jewels.
For as earth puts forth her growth,
And as a garden makes its sowing to spring forth,
So will Adonai Yahveh cause *His* righteous-dealing to spring forth,
And renown before all the nations.

For Zion's sake I will not be silent,
And for Jerusalem's sake I will not rest,
Till her prosperity go forth as brightness,

THE PROPHECIES OF ISAIAH.

Chapter LXII. 1—8.

And her deliverance like a torch that burns :
And *the* nations shall behold thy prosperity,
And all kings thy glory,
And men shall call thee by a new name,
Which Yahveh's mouth will appoint ;
And thou shalt become in Yahveh's hand a crown of adornment,
And a tiara of royalty in *the* hand of thine Elohim.
No more shalt thou be called ' Forsaken,'
And no more shall thy land be called ' Desolation,'
But thou shall be named ' My-delight-is-in-her '
And thy land " *The* Married ; "
For Yahveh delighteth in thee
And thy land will be married.
For as a youth marries a virgin,
Thy sons will marry thee ;
And *with* joy of bridegroom over bride,
Thine Elohim will joy over thee.

O Jerusalem ! I have stationed watchmen on thy walls ;
All the day and all the night they are never silent :
Rest not, ye remembrancers of Yahveh, nor give him rest,
Until he stablish and until he make Jerusalem a praise in *the* earth.
By his right hand, by arm of his strength hath Yahveh sworn,
Not again will I give thy corn *to be* food for thy foes,
Neither shall aliens drink thy new wine for which thou hast laboured :

Chapter LXII. 9—12.

But they who have harvested it shall eat it, and praise Yahveh,
And they who gather it in, shall drink it in my sacred courts,

Go through—go through *the* gates—
Prepare ye a way for the people :
Make high, make high the highway,
Clear it of stone—uplift a standard over the peoples.
Behold ! Yahveh has proclaimed unto *the* ends of the heart—
'Say ye to Zion's daughter, Behold thy deliverance comes ;
See ! his wage is with him and his recompense before him.'—
Then *men* call them ' The holy people, *the* released of Yahveh :'
And thou shalt be called ' Sought out '—' Unforsaken city.'

Chapter LXIII. 1.

The Downfall of Edom; a dialogue between the Prophet and Yahveh returning from Idumæa as a conqueror.

' Who *is* this that comes from Edom,
  In red attire from Bozrah ?
  This *that is* splendid in his raiment,
  With lofty bearing, in fulness of his strength ? '

CHAPTER LXIII. 1—6.

' I who announce *my* righteous-dealing,
Mighty to effect a rescue.'
' Why *the* redness on thy raiment,
And thy garments like his who treads in wine-press ? '
' Alone have I trodden *the* wine-trough,
And of peoples was no man with me :
So I trod them in my wrath
And trampled them in my fury,
And their life-juice besprinkled my garments,
And all my raiment have I soiled ;
For a day of vengance was in my heart,
And *the* year of my release had come,
And I looked—but no helper ;
And I was astounded—but no upholder.
My arm therefore wrought out a deliverance for me,
And my fury,—it upheld me ;
And I trod *the* peoples in my wrath
And broke them to pieces in my fury,
And poured their life-juice on *the* ground !'

CHAPTER LXIII. 7—LXIV. 1—12.

Thanksgivings, acknowledgments of divine mercy in the restoration, with confessions of sin.

CHAPTER LXIII. 7.

The kindness of Yahveh, Yahveh's praises will I celebrate,
According to all that Yahveh has bestowed upon us,

Chapter LXIII. 7.—14.

And, great goodness toward *the* house of Israel,
Which he bestowed on them according to his mercies,
And according to *the* greatness of his kindnesses.
'For,' said He, 'surely they are my people,
Sons who will not be faithless'—
And he became their deliverer.
In all their straits he was straitened,*
And an angel of his presence rescued them:
In his love and in his pity he himself released them,
And he lifted them up and carried them all *the* days of old.
Yet did they rebel and grieve his spirit of holiness,
So that he was changed to be their foe:—
Himself fought against them!

Then did his people remember *the* ancient days of Moses:
'Where,' *say they*, 'is He that brought them up out of *the* sea *with* the shepherds of his flock —
Where is He that put within him his Spirit of holiness?
He that made his glorious arm go forth at *the* right hand of Moses,
Cleaving waters before them,
To make himself a lasting name?
He that caused them to pass through deeps,
Like horses in *the* desert, without stumbling?
Like cattle which go down into a valley,
The spirit of Yahveh guided them;
Thus didst thou lead thy people
To make for thyself a name of glory.'

THE PROPHECIES OF ISAIAH. 165

CHAPTERS LXIII. 15—19.—LXV. 1—2.

Look from Heaven and behold,
From *the* abode of thy holiness and thy glory :
Where is thy jealousy and thy prowess ?
The yearning of thy bowels and thy compassions they have restrained themselves towards me !
For thou art our Father,
For Abraham takes no knowledge of us,
And Israel doth not own us !
Thou, Yahveh, art our Father,
Thy name from of old, ' our Vindicator.'
Why, Yahveh, cause us to err from thy ways—
Harden our heart from fearing thee ?
Return for thy servants' sake,
The tribes of thine inheritance :—
But a short time did thy holy people have possession ;
Our enemies have trodden down thy sanctuary ;
We have been *as* those over whom thou didst never rule,
Upon whom thy Name has not been called.

Oh that Thou wouldst rend *the* heavens,—wouldest descend—
That the mountains might quake before thee—
(As when fire kindles brushwood,
As when fire makes water to boil)
To make known thy name to thine enemies,
So *that* nations might tremble before thee,
When thou doest terrible things which we expected not,
When thou comest down *a d* mountains quake at thy presence !

CHAPTER LXIV. 2—11.

Even of old men had not heard, had not perceived by ear,
And eye had not seen, an Elohim beside thee,
Who would work for *him that* waiteth for him !
Thou meetest him who rejoices to do aright,
Who remember thee in thy ways.

Lo ! Thou wast wroth, and we had committed sins ;
We were of old in them, and can we be delivered ?
We all became as a thing unclean,
And all our righteous deeds like a menstruous garment ;
And we all withered like leaves,
And our sins like a blast, carried us away :
And there is none that calls on thy name,
That bestirs himself to lay hold on thee ;
For thou hidest thy face from us,
And causest us to pine away through our sins.

Yet now, Yahveh, our Father Thou !
We the clay, and thou our potter,
And we are all *the* work of thy hands :
O Yahveh, be not exceeding wroth, nor remember iniquity for ever ;
Lo ! see now, we *are* all thy people !
Thy Holy cities have become a wilderness—
Zion has become a wilderness, Jerusalem a desolation :
Our house of holiness and splendour where our fathers praised thee,
Has become a burning of fire,

CHAPTER LXIV. 12.
And all our much loved places have come to ruin.
Yahveh, wilt thou refrain thyself at these things?
Wilt thou keep silence, and afflict us very sore?

CHAPTERS LXV. LXVI.
The return of relapsed Israelites, with mingled cautions against idolatry, and promises of spiritual prosperity: The diffusion of the Faith and its perpetuity. . . .
[*These concluding chapters have no connection with what precedes, and refer to a state of Palestinian life subsequent to the Exile.*]

CHAPTER LXV. 1—4.
I have been sought out by those who asked not *of me*,
By them that inquired not of me, am I found :
I said, 'I am here, I am here,'
To a nation that called not on my name.
All the day did I spread out my hands to a revolting people,
Who walk in the way that is not good, after their own devices ;
The people that ever provoke me to my face,
Sacrificing in gardens,
And burning incense upon the *altar* bricks ;
Who sit in tombs and lodge in secret places,

Chapter LXV. 4—11.

Who eat flesh of the swine
And broth of unclean meats *is in* their vessels ;
Who say, ' Keep to thyself, come not near me,
For I am holy unto thee.'
A smoke in my nostrils, these,
A fire that smoulders all the day !
Behold ! it is written before me, ' I will not be silent,
Except I requite, even requite into their bosom.
Your sins and the sins of your fathers together, saith Yahveh,
Who burned incense upon the mountains,
And put me to scorn upon the hills !'
Therefore I mete out their former demerit into their bosom.

Thus saith Yahveh :
As when the grape-juice is found in a cluster,
And one saith, ' Destroy it not, for a blessing is therein,'
So will I act for my servants' sake that I destroy not the whole :
And I will bring forth a seed out of Jacob,
And from Judah an inheritor of my mountains,
And my chosen shall inherit them, and my servants dwell there ;
And the Sharon will be a fold for sheep,
And *the* valley of Achor a resting-place for cattle,
For my people who sought me.

But as for you who forsake Yahveh,
Who forget my holy mountain—

THE PROPHECIES OF ISAIAH.

CHAPTER LXV. 11—18.

Who prepare a table for Fortune,
And who fill a libation to Destiny,
You I destine to the sword ;*
And ye shall all bow down to slaughter,
Because I called and ye answered not,
I spoke but ye did not hear,
But did what was evil in mine eyes,
And chose that wherein I had no pleasure.
Therefore thus saith Adonai Yahveh :
Lo, my servants shall eat, but ye shall hunger ;
Lo, my servants shall drink, but ye shall thirst ;
Lo, my servants shall rejoice, but ye shall be ashamed ;
Lo, my servants shall shout for joy of heart,
But ye shall cry aloud for grief of heart,
And ye shall wail for brokenness of spirit.
And ye shall leave your name for an imprecation to my
    chosen,
—' So may Adonai Yahveh slay thee '—
But he will call his servants by another name,
So that he in *the* land who blesses himself,
Will bless himself by *the* Elohim of faithfulness,
And he in *the* land who swears,
Will swear by *the* Elohim of faithfulness,
Because the former troubles are forgotten,
And because they are hidden from mine eyes.

For lo ! I create new heavens and a new earth,
And the former things shall be forgotten,
And shall not come up to mind.
Rejoice ye rather, and exult for ever at what I create ;

Chapters LXV. 18.—LXVI. 1.

For lo, I create Jerusalem an exultation and her people a joy,
And I exult in Jerusalem and rejoice in my people:
No more shall be heard therein voice of wailing and voice of outcry:
No more shall there be thence an infant of a *few* days,
Or old man who cannot fill up his days;
For the youth shall die the son of a hundred years,
But the sinner, son of a hundred years, shall be accursed.
And they shall build houses and inhabit *them*,
And plant vineyards and eat their fruit:
They shall not build and another inhabit;
They shall not plant and another eat;
For *the* days of my people shall be as *the* days of a tree,
And my chosen shall wear out *the* work of their hands.
Not for vanity shall they labour
Nor bring forth *children* for calamity,
For they are a seed of *the* blessed of Yahveh,
And their offspring with them.
And it shall come to pass that ere yet they call, I will anwser,
While they are yet speaking, I will hear:
Wolf and lamb will pasture together,
And a lion eat straw like an ox,
And *as for* a serpent—dust shall be his food!
They will not harm nor destroy, has Yahveh said,
In all my holy mountain.
Thus saith Yahveh:
The heavens are my throne and the earth my footstool:
What manner of house will ye build for me?

CHAPTER LXVI. 1—6.

And what manner of place for my rest ?
For all these things my hand hath made,
And all these *thus* came to be ;—an utterance of Yahveh ;—
But on this man will I look,
On *the* sufferer and bruised in spirit,
And who trembles at my word.

He who slaughters the ox—kills a man !
He who sacrifices the lamb—breaks a dog's neck !
He who offers up a minchah—*it is* swine's blood !
He who makes a memorial of incense—blesses evil !
Even as they have chosen their ways,
And their soul delights in their abominations,
I too will choose their misfortunes,
And I will bring their fears upon them,
Because I called and no one answered.
I spoke and they would not hear,
But did that which was evil in mine eyes
And chose that in which I delighted not.

Hear *the* word of Yahveh,
Ye who tremble at his word :
Your brethren that hate you,
That cast you out on account of my name, say,
' Let Yahveh glorify himself, that we may look upon your joy,'
But they shall be ashamed.

A voice of roaring from *the* city—

Chapter LXVI. 6—14.

A voice from *the* Temple!
A voice of Yahveh rendering recompense to his foes!

' Ere she travailed she brought forth;
Ere her throes came on her, she was delivered of a man-child!
Who has heard the like? who has seen such things?
Can a land be brought forth in a single day?
Can a nation be born at once?
For Zion travailed—also brought forth her sons!'
Should I bring to the birth, and not cause to bring forth, saith Yahveh?
Should I who beget, hinder? saith thine Elohim.

Rejoice with Jerusalem, and exult in her all ye that love her;
Joy with her joyously, all ye who mourned over her;
That ye may suck and be satisfied from *the* breast of her consolations;
That ye may press out with delight from *the* fulness of her glory:
For thus saith Yahveh:
Behold, I extend peace to her like a river,
And *the* glory of *the* nations like a swelling torrent,
And ye shall suck therefrom and be borne upon *the* side,
And on *the* knees shall ye be fondled;
As one whom his mother comforts, so will I comfort you,
And in Jerusalem shall ye be comforted.
And when ye see it your heart rejoices,
And your bones flourish like young grass,

CHAPTER LXVI. 14—20.

And Yahveh's hand becomes known to his servants,
But with his enemies he is wrathful.
For see! Yahveh comes in fire,
And his chariots are like a whirlwind,
Causing his anger to return with fury,
And his rebuke with flames of fire :
For by fire will Yahveh judge,
And by his sword, with all flesh,
And many shall be *the* slain of Yahveh.
They who consecrate and cleanse themselves
For the gardens, after one *standing* in the midst,
Who eat swine's flesh and the abomination and the mouse—
Together shall they perish. *It is the* utterance of Yahveh.

But *I know* their deeds and their thoughts :
The time is come to gather all the nations and the tongues,
And they shall come and behold my glory.
For I will set up a sign among them :
And the escaped of them will I send to the nations ;
To Tarshish and Pul who draw *the* bow,
To Tubal and Javan, to the far off countries,
That have not heard the report of me or seen my glory ;
And they shall declare my glory among *the* nations,
And shall bring all your brethren,
From all the nations for an oblation to Yahveh,
On horses and in chariots and in litters,
On mules and on dromedaries,
To my holy hill, to Jerusalem, saith Yahveh,

CHAPTER LXVI. 20—24.

Even as *the* sons of Israel bring the oblation,
In a pure vessel to Yahveh's house ;
And of them will I also take for priests, for Levites, saith Yahveh.
For as the new heavens and the new earth which I make,
Stand before me—*it is the* utterance of Yahveh—
So shall your seed and your name stand :
And it comes to pass that from new moon to new moon,
And from Sabbath to Sabbath,
All flesh will come to worship before me, saith Yahveh,
And they will go forth and gaze upon *the* carcases of the men who rebelled against me :
For their worm shall not die,
And their fire shall not be quenched,
And to all flesh shall they be an abhorrence.

THE END.

www.ingramcontent.com/pod-product-compliance
Lightning Source LLC
Chambersburg PA
CBHW031439160426

43195CB00010BB/785